BRICK HISTORY

BRICK HISTORY

AMAZING HISTORICAL SCENES TO BUILD FROM LEGO®

WARREN ELSMORE

A Quintet Book

First published in Great Britain in 2016 by
The History Press
The Mill
Brimscombe Port
Stroud
Gloucestershire
GL5 2QG
U.K.

www.thehistorypress.co.uk

ISBN 978-0-7509-6757-0
QTT.BHIS

This book was conceived, designed and produced by
Quintet Publishing Limited
114–116 Western Road
Hove, East Sussex
BN3 1DD
United Kingdom

Photographer: Michael Wolchover
Designer: Gareth Butterworth
Art Director: Michael Charles
Project Editor: Caroline Elliker
Publisher: Mark Searle

Additional photography:
118, 120–121, 180 Alex Eylar
130, 132–133 Erik Platt
150, 152 Michael Evans
172–177 Gary Brooks
188 Ricky Rhodes
14–15, 46–47, 244–247 Simon Pickard

10 9 8 7 6 5 4 3 2 1
Printed in China by Toppan Leefung

Contents

WELCOME TO *BRICK HISTORY*!

In *Brick City* we explored the world's architecture. *Brick Wonders* delved into the most amazing things that have ever been created. *Brick Vehicles* looked at everything that moved. So, where to next? Back into history, of course!

Brick History is a whistle-stop tour of the last 13.8 billion years, from the Big Bang all the way to the modern day (though, truth be told, we don't include much from the first 13 billion years!). In this book, I use LEGO® bricks to recreate some of the most iconic moments in time, whether they are changes in the way we look at ourselves or changes in the natural world.

When we started to plan *Brick History*, we were a little concerned that it might turn into one long book full of battles and wars. Sometimes when we think of history, it's the really big events that stand out in our minds. Looking more closely, though, it soon became apparent that some of the most significant moments in our history started out very small. Take the discovery of the vaccination against smallpox, for instance. This 'small' discovery changed the world more (and saved more lives) than any war prior – or since.

In *Brick History*, we've identified about 70 key moments in our history. We begin with the start of everything – the Big Bang. Then, we move on through to prehistory and the dawn of civilisation. In the first chapter, we also look at the explosion of trade, the increase in knowledge and the start of modern politics.

Our second chapter covers the next two big leaps in the way we live our lives. The Renaissance period gave us amazing art, technological inventions and a new understanding of how the world works. Next was the period of empire. Britain, along with other European nations, developed empires stretching from the Far East to Africa, and onwards to the Americas. The same period also saw the independence of the United States.

In the third chapter, our world really gets moving! There are still battles to be won in the nineteenth century, but there are also railway tracks to be laid, there's gold to be found, and massive scientific discoveries to be made. This is also the time of great change in the United States, as the Civil War brought about an end to slavery.

The final chapter brings us right up to the present. It's only in the twentieth century that we finally see the recognition of equality and rights throughout the world. Walls crumble and people begin making their own decisions. We leave the ground, take to the skies in aeroplanes and then leave this planet altogether as the space race begins!

Hopefully, you enjoy this short trip with me through our shared history. Perhaps you'll be inspired by some of the models and try building them at home yourself. Perhaps you'll be inspired by some of the adventurers, inventors and scientists we look at and want to follow in their footsteps. Or perhaps, in a few years' time, someone like me will write a book about your amazing achievements and how you changed the world.

Whatever you do, I hope you enjoy the book and – as always – have fun building!

PRACTICE PROJECT

It's time to limber up those LEGO®-building fingers with a practice project! This model is the lifeboat from the *Titanic* scene.

Building a small boat from LEGO bricks is not an easy task. A boat's hull is smoothly curved, while of course LEGO bricks have sharp corners. However, in this build I've used the curved slope pieces to create the illusion of a smooth hull. Using these pieces gave me a second problem, though, as they needed to be mounted sideways in order to follow the correct curve. Thankfully, The LEGO Group has recently released a few new pieces that work perfectly for this model.

The 'bracket' is an essential LEGO piece for mounting bricks on their sides or straight up. The design of the piece is actually very clever. While the top is the thickness of a standard plate, the side part is only ½ plate thick. This might seem strange, until you remember the geometry of the LEGO bricks. A 2 x 2 LEGO brick is 5 plates wide. That means a 1 x 1 brick is 2½ plates wide. Using a bracket means that you can mount 2 LEGO plates on their sides and the result will be exactly the same width as one brick.

Take a look throughout the book and see if you can spot where we've used this special geometry to follow the shapes of real items.

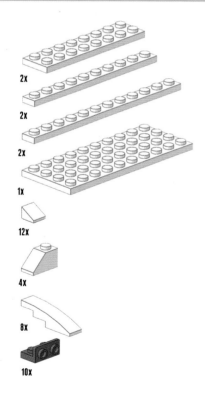

2x

2x

2x

1x

12x

4x

8x

10x

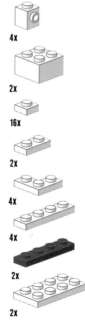

4x

2x

16x

2x

4x

4x

2x

2x

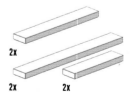

2x

2x

2x

2x

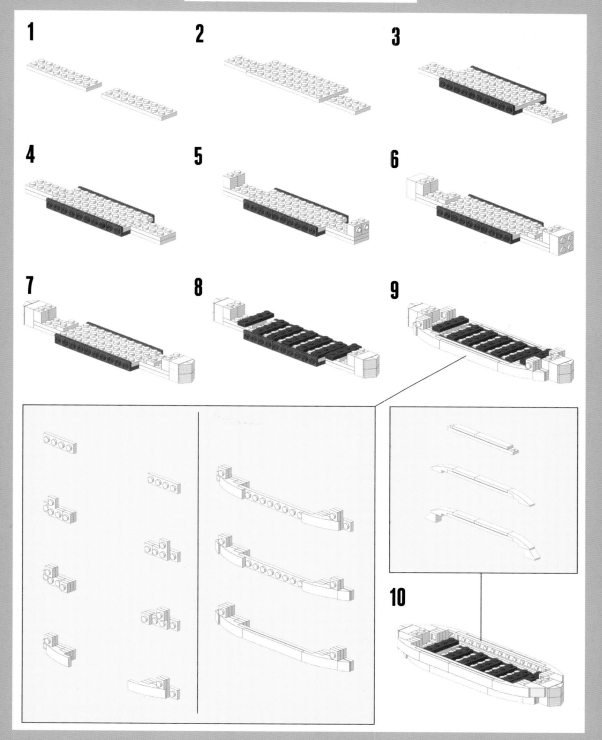

PHOTOGRAPHING YOUR MODELS

One of the best ways to keep a permanent record of your LEGO® models is to take photographs of them. But because LEGO bricks can be difficult to photograph, I'll give you some tips for how to take that great photo.

The good news is that you don't really need any special camera equipment to take photos of LEGO models – just some patience and a few pointers. Let's start with a camera that we all may have – the one on your phone, or a very simple point-and-shoot camera.

The key to good LEGO photography is not the camera, but the light – and this is especially important when you can't adjust anything on the camera itself. To get a good picture of your model, you'll want to find somewhere with good light – perhaps the kitchen or even outdoors on a sunny day. Next, so that your model stands out, try to have a nice blank background. Something as simple as a sheet, neatly laid out, can make a huge difference. Don't worry about it being white, either – some models look great on coloured backgrounds.

Once your model is ready to be photographed, try taking a test shot and see how it looks. If it's still dark – or your picture looks grainy – you might need more light. Try to find something like a desk lamp, but remember, if you point the desk light directly at your model, it will probably reflect back right into your camera. Black LEGO bricks are really great at doing this, but it will make for a horrible photo! Try to point the lamp at the ceiling and bounce the light back down onto the model and see if things improve.

If your picture is still not great, or is blurred, then it's possible that your camera is moving while you are taking the photograph. The best thing to fix this is a small tripod. It doesn't have to be an expensive one – you could even make a stand for your camera out of LEGO bricks. All that's important is that it keeps your camera still when it takes the picture.

So, that's the basics. Now, what if you have a camera with more advanced options? Well, all of the above still applies (especially the lighting and the tripod), but if you have a camera with scene modes, then it's certainly worth trying these. Something like a macro or still-life mode is best to try first.

If you're lucky enough to have a camera with a full manual mode, or aperture priority modes, then you should be able to get some really good pictures. Remember that because your model won't move as the camera will be fixed on a tripod, you can have the shutter open for as long as you need. Try setting a really high aperture number for some sharp images.

And, if you know all of this already, then I'll mention just one more thing to you – a circular polarising filter. It's quite a complex thing to explain, but we use one on almost every single photograph in the book and it can make a huge difference in the quality of your image. Remember, though, that whatever equipment you're using to take the photograph is not as important as the thing in front of the camera. So don't worry too much about it – just keep on building awesome models!

How to Clean Your LEGO® Bricks

One question that I'm constantly being asked is how to clean LEGO bricks. I'll admit that it gives me a little pause for thought – you see, I don't clean mine!

While that sounds horrible, there's a very good reason why I don't clean my LEGO bricks – they never get dirty. Because I build LEGO models every day for a living, I'm very lucky that almost every brick I use is brand new – these bricks have never been out of the box (or at least not for very long!). I'm also very careful when I build because of all the photographs that we take. No eating for me when I'm building, and I always have to make sure that my hands are really clean.

Although I don't have to clean my bricks, I do know how you should clean them. If you buy bricks second hand (which is a great way to get LEGO), or if the bricks have been around for a while, you may want to make sure that they are in tip-top condition.

The first – and most important – step is to decide what LEGO elements you have. Nearly everything LEGO makes can be easily cleaned, but there are some very important exceptions. The first exception is ANYTHING with metal in it. That includes train tracks, wheels with metal axles and of course anything electrical (motors, wires, battery boxes etc.). The second exception is any pieces that have stickers on them. You're going to need to clean these separately.

As for the standard bricks, the easiest way to clean these is by washing them. They're plastic and can deal pretty well with water. The best way to wash them is by hand in some warm, soapy water. Get hold of a soft brush and give them a scrub (probably not the one you use for washing dishes, though) – the bricks should come out just fine. Keep the temperature under 40°C (104°F) for both the LEGO bricks' sake and your own.

If you have a lot of bricks, you might be tempted to use the dishwasher or washing machine. While LEGO doesn't recommend it, I've heard that lots of people do this. Just make sure that the temperature is very low and that there's no way for the bricks to escape. There are some very small LEGO pieces that might do your machine damage, so make sure that first, you have permission to use the machine, and second, you protect the machine. Put your bricks into something like an old pillowcase or a delicates bag to make sure that they can't escape.

Once washed, it's best to leave the elements to air dry. Put them somewhere warm if you can, and every so often move them around. Sometimes LEGO bricks take a long time to dry out, but be patient. Wet LEGO bricks don't make good models!

As for those other bricks, you have a decision to make. If you wash bricks with stickers on, you're likely to end up with just bricks. Putting anything with metal in it underwater will probably cause it to rust, and if it's an electric part, it will fail altogether. What I'd suggest is to carefully clean the plastic parts with a damp cloth or maybe a little gentle cleanser. Just don't use a cream cleanser, otherwise, your bricks will scratch.

MODEL TECHNIQUES

You might notice that a few of the models in this book employ some clever techniques. Some of our topics are huge – really huge – and it's just not possible to build LEGO® models that have all the detail that we want at the scale that we want. So, how do we make people think that they do?

There are some well-known techniques that builders and artists use to fool people into thinking something is real – and most of these work just as well using LEGO bricks!

Forced perspective is one old trick. It works by mimicking the real world. When you see something close to you, it appears bigger, whereas something further away appears smaller. So, if you want to make something look like it's further away, you can build a smaller model of it. If it's very far away, even a really big thing (such as a ship) would appear quite small.

I've used the forced perspective technique in the Spanish Armada scene (pages 96–99). The Spanish Armada consisted of hundreds of huge galleons. We simply would never have enough space to build this in our studio. In addition, we wanted to include the famous scene of Sir Walter Raleigh playing bowls. If we built all these things on the same scale, then it would be very difficult to highlight him. The galleons are only slightly smaller than Sir Walter, but they are also placed slightly into the background. This forces your perspective – you know that the galleons are actually huge, so your mind tells you that they must just be a very long way away to appear so small. The same goes for the Thermopylae battle scene on page 14, with the smaller figures in the distance along the cliff top.

Another trick I've used in this book and all my others is a technique called selective compression. You will have seen the most famous use of this technique without even realising it – and probably not where you expect. If you've ever seen photos of an amusement park – or been to one yourself – then you would have probably been impressed by the huge buildings on the grounds. Houses have lots of floors and castles seem enormous. Except… they aren't.

When building a model, it's often important to include certain key parts, and to do that, you need to exclude others. Or perhaps if you create the model correctly, it would be too large to build or move around (or you might not have enough LEGO bricks!). This is where selective compression comes in. Take a look at the Pompeii scene on page 54, for instance. In real life, the volcano Vesuvius is quite far from Pompeii – it appears on the horizon. However, in order to express the magnitude of the eruption and the devastation it brought to the Roman town, I've compressed that distance. Sure, it's not 100 percent accurate, but it really gives the impression of the disaster that happened.

Trompe-l'œil is another very old art technique. In this instance, it uses a two-dimensional image (such as a painting or drawing) to reflect a three-dimensional object. I've used a variation of this technique in the painting of the Sistine Chapel on page 82. I wanted Michelangelo as a minifigure, but this posed a problem because if I did that, then the actual chapel roof would be far too small to model in LEGO. Instead, I had a real artist draw a version of the chapel roof that Michelangelo was painting. To further the illusion, I included real scaffolding for him to sit on. The other trick here is how we photographed the model. It simply wouldn't have been practical to get underneath the scaffolding to get the correct angle, so we did the next best thing and turned the whole model upside down. Once the photograph was taken, it was impossible to know which way it was shot.

THE BATTLE OF THERMOPYLAE, 480 B.C.E.

Fought over three days during the second Persian invasion of Greece, this famous battle took place when Persian general Xerxes led his army and navy across the coastal pass of Thermopylae – "The Hot Gates" – where they were stopped by the Athenian army of Greece, led by King Leonidas of Sparta, and famously held off for seven days. The Greeks were eventually overwhelmed by the much larger Persian army, with the help of a Greek traitor. This courageous effort on the part of the Greeks has been reenacted twice in Hollywood, the most recent being in the 2006 film *300*.

PREHISTORY AND THE BIRTH OF CIVILISATION

THE BIG BANG

We start our story at the very beginning – 13.8 billion years ago. Through measurements of the universe, we know that it is expanding as it grows. Working backwards, scientists such as Stephen Hawking developed the theory that the universe started out as a single point, or singularity. The universe has been continually expanding since the Big Bang, and we can trace every galaxy, star, planet and moon back to that point. Of course, no one really knows what happened when the Big Bang occurred, so we've created an illustration of what such an explosion might have looked like. It has taken more than 32,000 pieces to create this picture – a mosaic measuring more than 2m (6.5ft) wide!

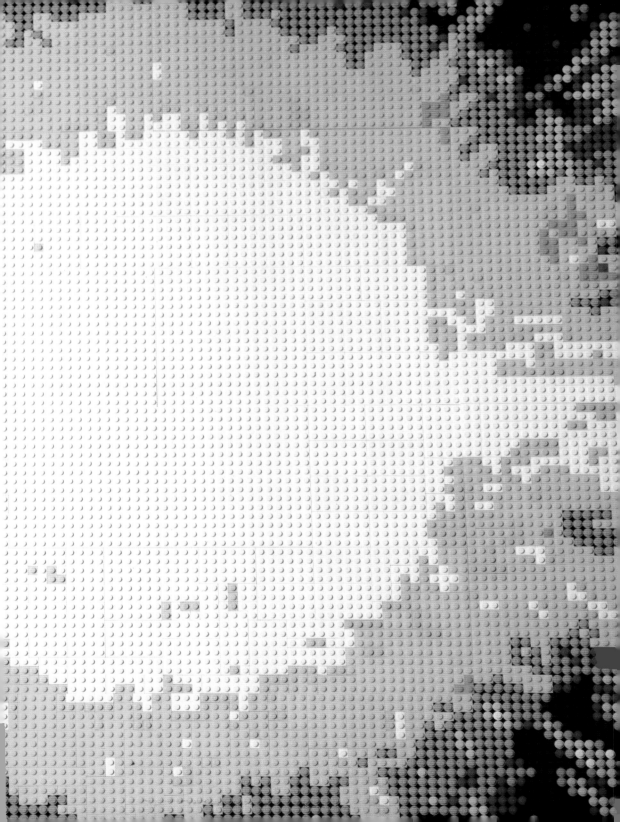

DINOSAUR EXTINCTION

You might think that the human race has been on this planet for quite some time, but that's nothing compared to the rule of the dinosaurs. For 135 million years, this group of animals was in charge! Ranging from creatures no bigger than a pigeon to some that weighed more than 60 tons, many different beings lived on Earth that no longer exist today.

It is believed that around 66 million years ago a huge meteorite hit the Earth, either cooling the planet by throwing dust into the atmosphere or causing a huge heatwave. This change in climate was enough to cause many of the dinosaurs to die out. Not all of them, though—some creatures from that period are still with us, ranging from insects to crocodiles!

Lascaux Cave Paintings

In southwestern France, there is a cave. Nothing unique about that – except that in this cave there are paintings all over the walls. The paintings are very special, as they are more than 17,000 years old, and were drawn by people who are believed to have been living in or around the caves at the time. The majority of the paintings depict animals that would have lived alongside the people, or been hunted by them. Horses, deer and bison are present, alongside big cats, birds, bears and even a rhinoceros. In order to preserve this ancient graffiti, the caves are now closed to the public. However, if you visit that part of the world, you can see a recreation of the caves and wonder at them yourself.

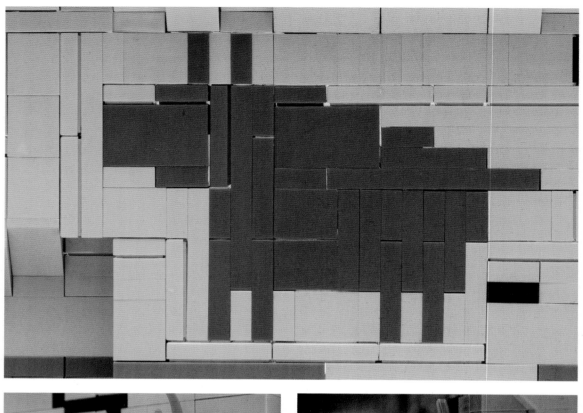

INVENTION OF THE WHEEL, c.3500 B.C.E.

No one really knows exactly when the wheel was invented, but the earliest evidence of wheeled vehicles comes from more than 6,000 years ago. Wheels were in use well before then, though, for at least 3,000 years. Contrary to Hollywood films, making a wheel is not as simple as chopping a slice out of a tree! So that the wheel can take the weight properly, it's necessary to make it from planks of wood. The very first wheels were solid, like our cart, with spoked wheels coming almost 2,000 years later. It wasn't until the late nineteenth century that the pneumatic tyre was introduced, making the ride much more comfortable!

1

2

3

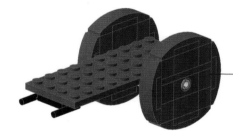

THE FIRST CLOCK, c.3500 B.C.E.

Did you know that you can tell the time with LEGO® bricks? Although you could probably build a modern clock with LEGO Technic pieces, there is a much simpler way! The Egyptian shadow clock is one of the simplest and earliest methods of telling the time. To tell the time, you need to place the base so that it's facing east/west. First, you need the morning sun to calibrate it. As the sun moves overhead, you'll see a shadow projected on the base. Mark off each hour on the scale. When you get to midday (no shadow), turn it around through 180 degrees and it should now read the afternoon hours. Once calibrated, you can use it every day — though, perhaps a watch is easier!

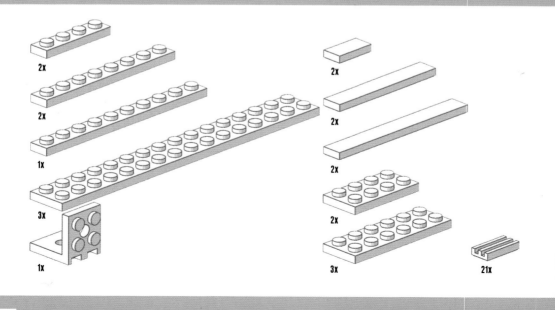

2x

2x

1x

3x

1x

2x

2x

2x

2x

3x

21x

1

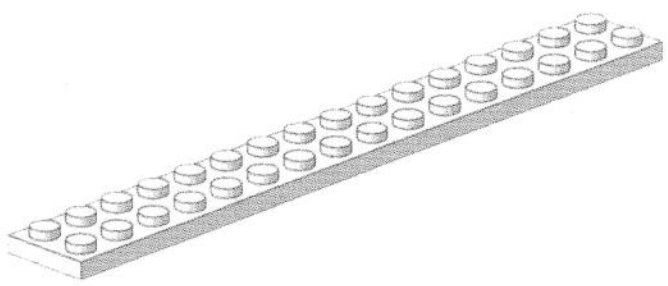

2

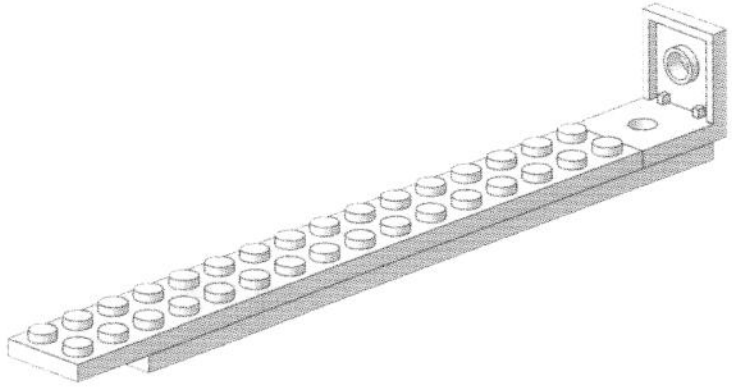

3

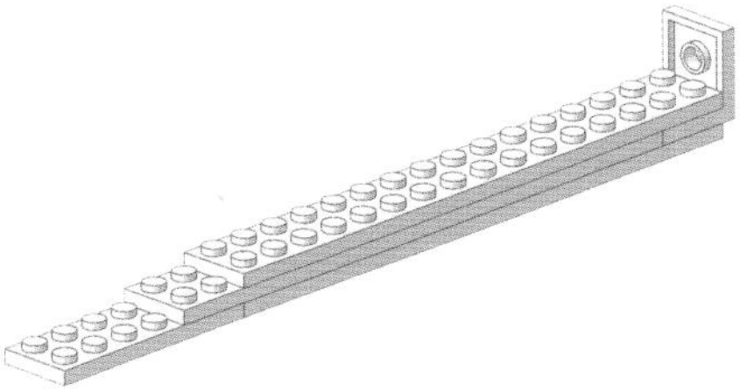

4

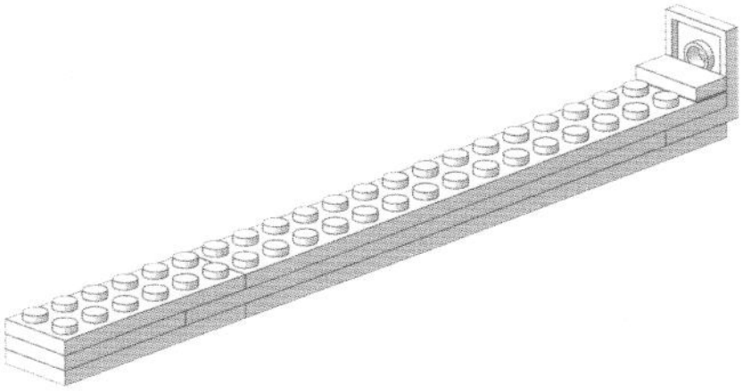

5

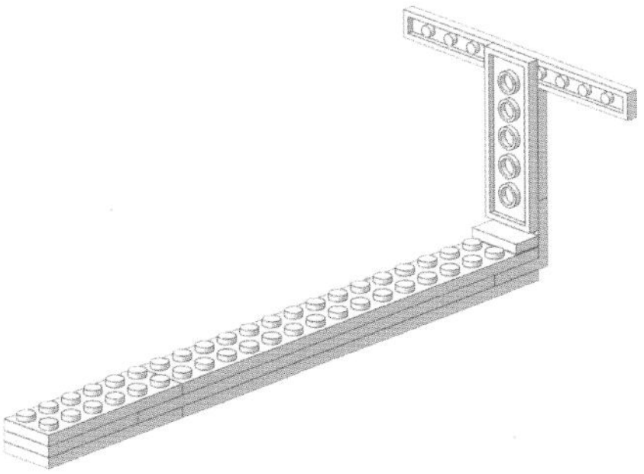

6

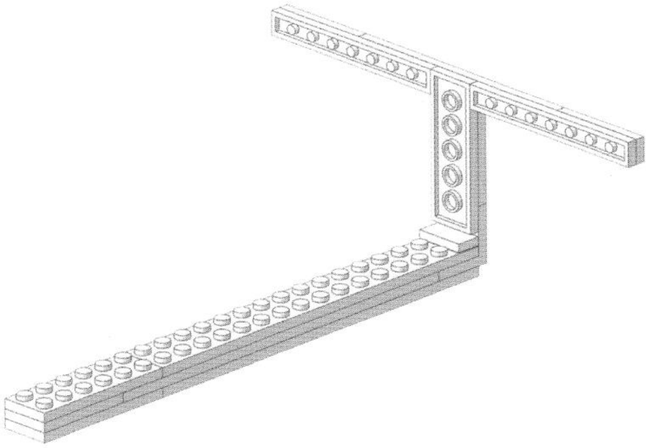

7

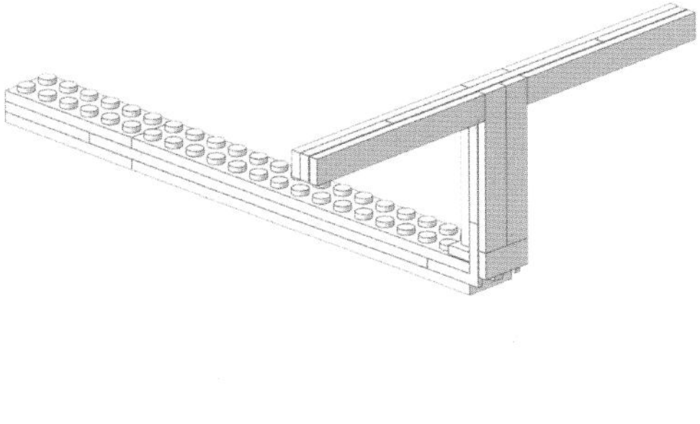

8

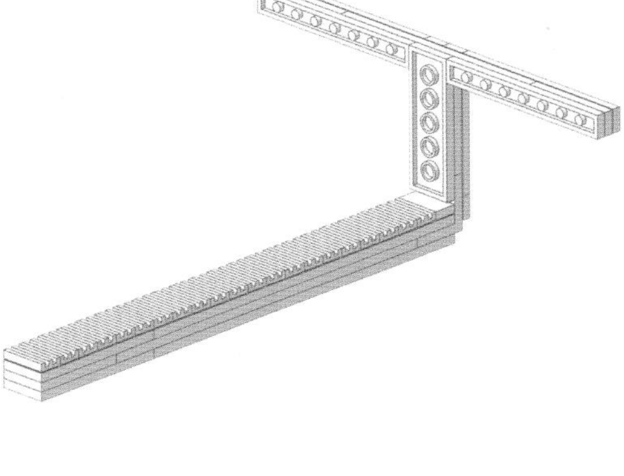

ATHENIAN DEMOCRACY, C.500 B.C.E.

What we understand today as democracy (making decisions by a vote) first started way back in ancient Greece. The word first appeared in Athens around 500 B.C.E. When major decisions were made, a huge group of people was assembled – sometimes up to 60,000 people were present! By modern standards, though, democracy was limited. You were only allowed to speak or vote in this assembly if you were male, older than 20 years of age, not a slave, and a landowner. To guide this assembly, a council of 400 people was formed as an executive committee. Debating and public speaking were held in very high regard in Greek society, and were essential skills to have if you wanted a career in politics or even just to defend yourself. There were no lawyers back then – it was up to each citizen to present his own case.

THE FIRST OLYMPICS, 776 B.C.E.

The very first Olympics were run by the ancient Greeks in 776 B.C.E. and were a very different event than the modern games. The ancient games included some recognisable events such as sprints, wrestling, javelin, and boxing – as well as chariot racing and fighting competitions. Our model is of a discobolus, or a discus thrower. It's a famous sculpture dating from around 450 B.C.E. Although the original statue no longer exists, it has been copied throughout the centuries in bronze, marble and now LEGO® bricks! Looking at the original statue, you might notice one big difference between the ancient athletes and their modern counterparts. In ancient Greece, it was normal for athletes to compete entirely nude!

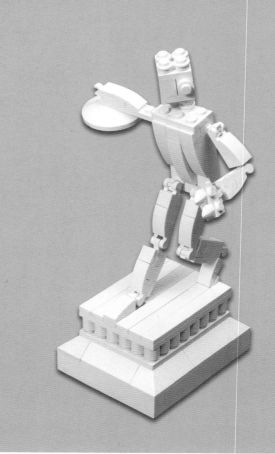

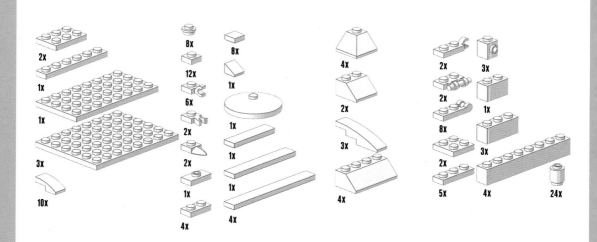

1

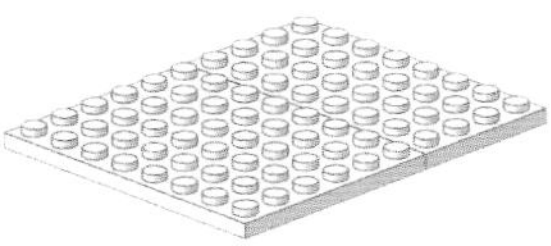

2

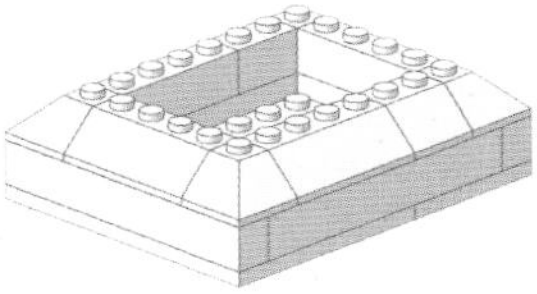

3

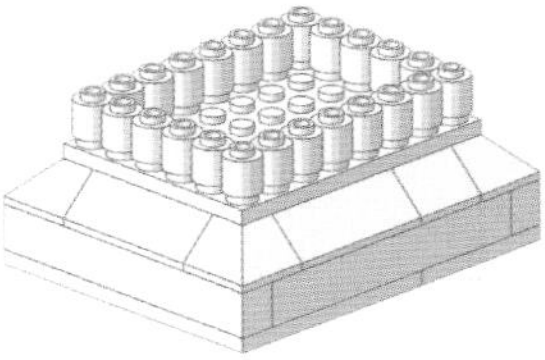

4

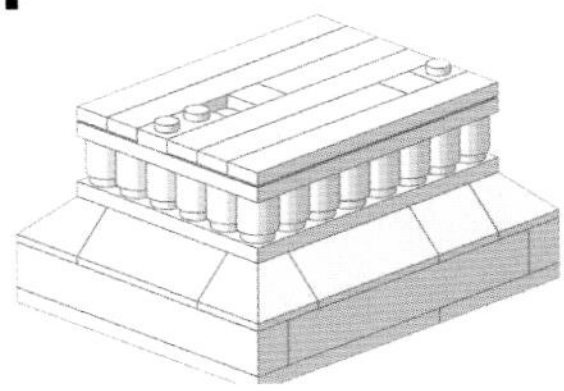

5

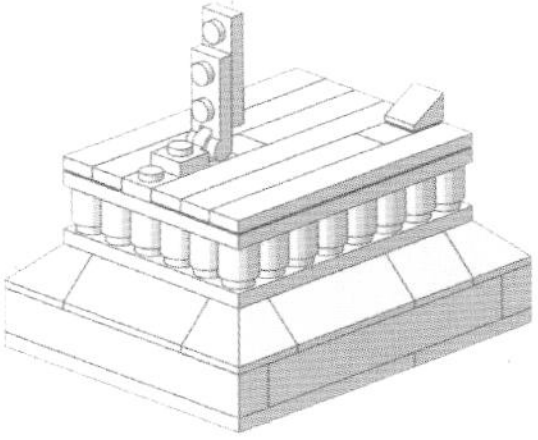

6

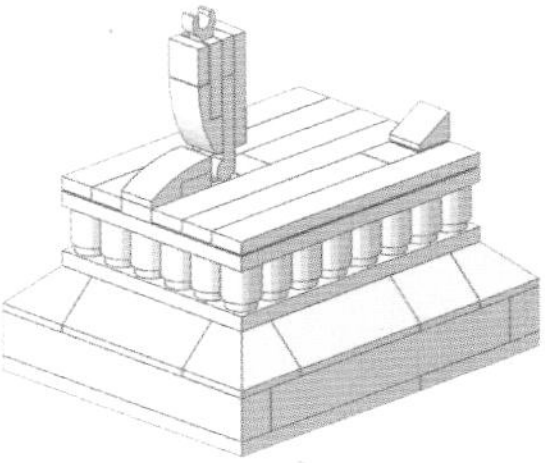

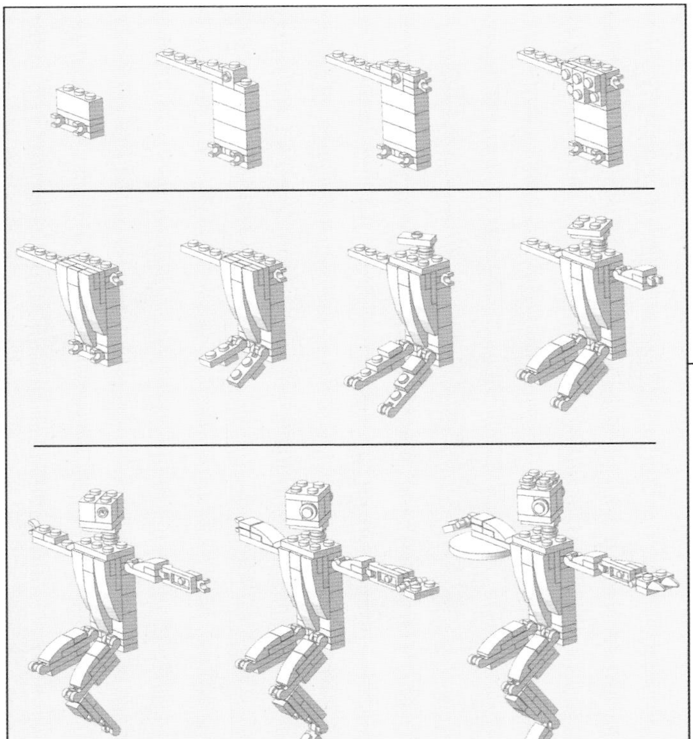

7

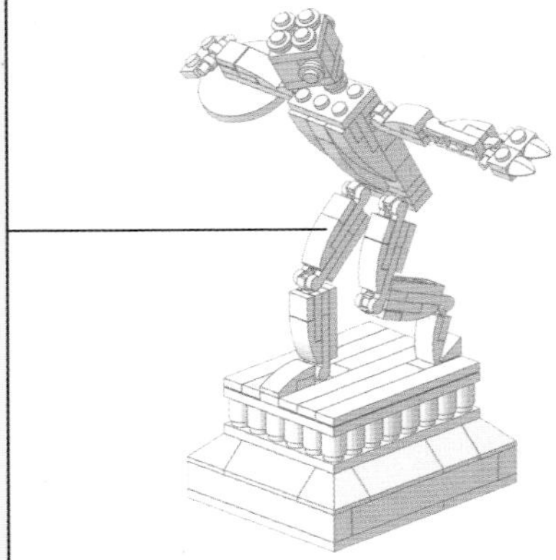

THE FIRST SILK ROUTE, 206 B.C.E.

Many things that we use in our modern lives were first developed in China – silk being just one of them! Early travellers to China discovered this wonderful fabric, but they knew its real value would be found if they brought it back to Europe. The transport of this first import gave the road its name – The Silk Route. Traders would buy silk in the Far East and transport it 6,500km (4,000 miles) back home. More importantly, although they took the silk home, these travellers also brought these countries many things as well, such as art and religion. It was the silk routes that first started the mixing of people from around the world – something that has continued to this day. In fact, the silk routes are still in use – they have just moved from horses on dirt tracks to container ships on the sea, and carry televisions and other modern goods rather than silk!

Early Maps and Alphabets

Did you know that many of the first cartographers were Chinese? Maps have been discovered in China that date back to around 400 B.C.E. And Chinese writing has been in use for more than 2,000 years, but is very different than that used in many Western countries. In the Arabic alphabet used in Western countries, each letter is represented by a single symbol such as 'A', but Chinese characters represent a syllable of a word or often an entire word. This means learning to write is much harder. Most educated Chinese are able to write around 4,000 symbols. However, creating an accurate representation of a Chinese character in straight-sided LEGO® bricks is a challenge! This model uses bricks in all directions and some clever geometry to make it all fit together. In case you were wondering, this, of course, is the symbol for 'brick'.

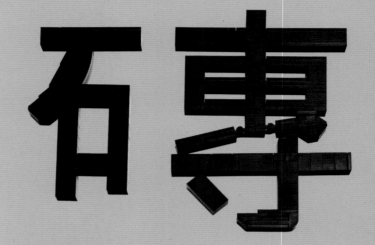

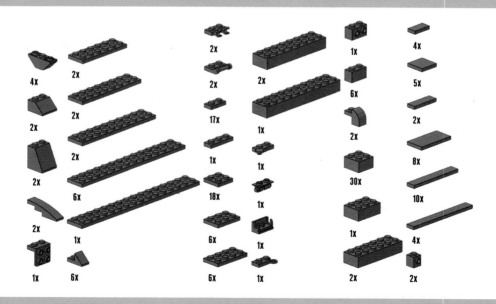

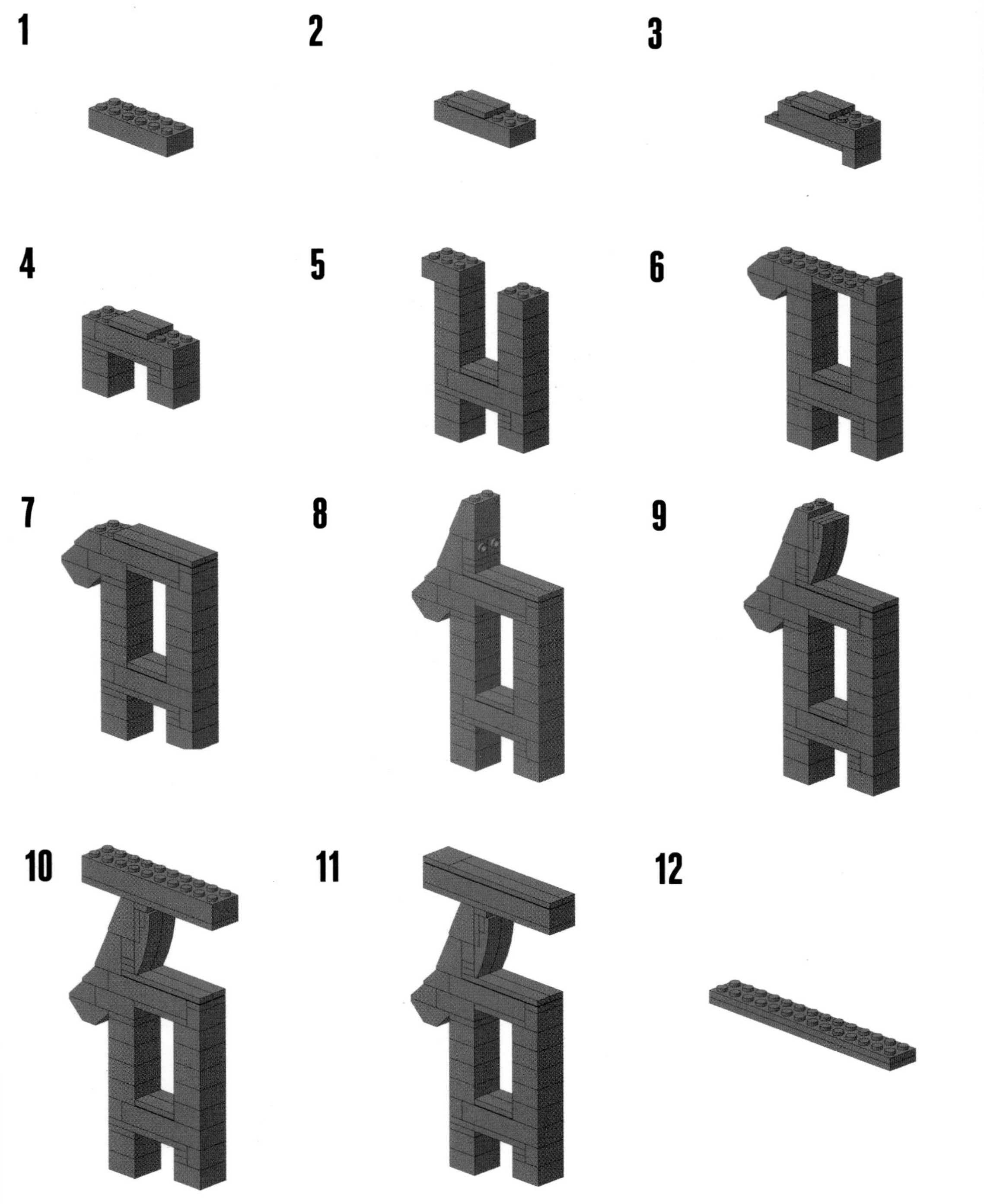

1

2

3

4

5

6

7

8

9

10

11

12

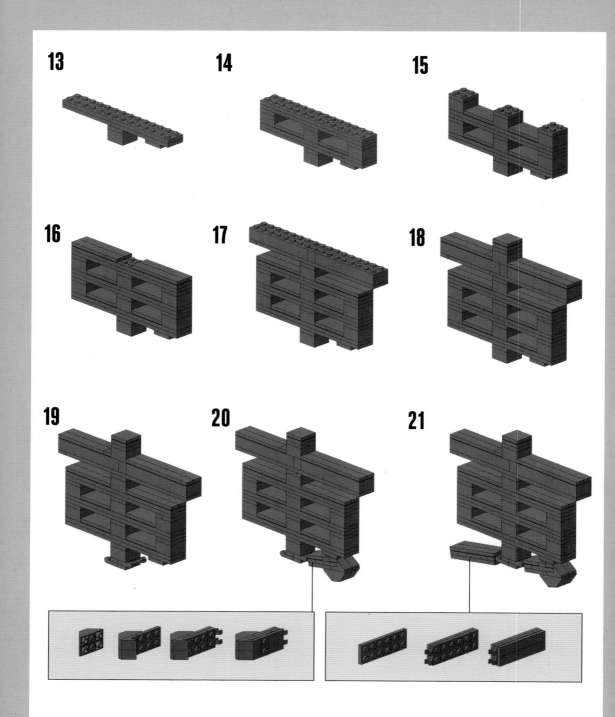

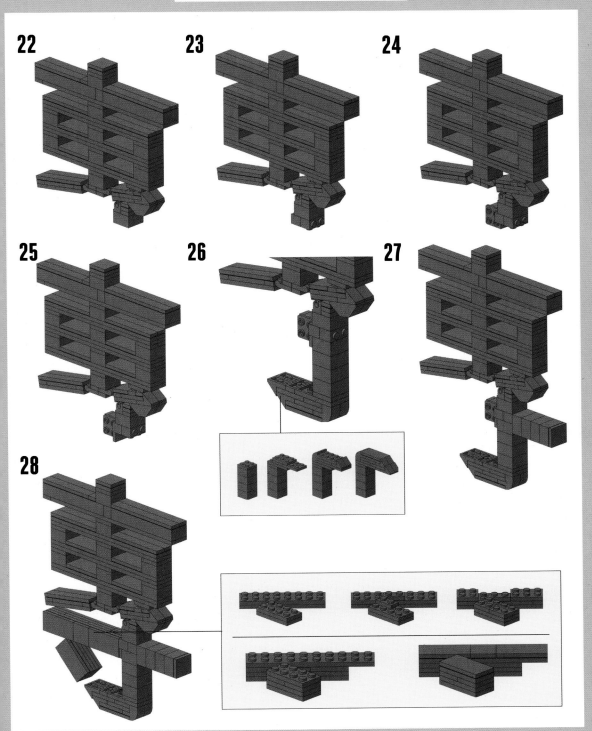

CONSTRUCTION OF THE TERRACOTTA ARMY, 246–206 B.C.E.

The rites and rituals associated with death vary all over the world and often change with time. Just as the Egyptians buried their pharaohs in huge pyramids, the ancient Chinese had similar reverence for their emperors. When alive, the Chinese rulers would have had huge armies to protect them, so why not do the same for the afterlife? The Terracotta Army is an army built especially to protect Qin Shi Huang, the first Emperor of China. In what must have been a unique project, more than 8,000 warriors, 500 horses and 100 chariots were made out of clay. Each statue was individually assembled by hand and then buried near the emperor's tomb to keep him safe in the next life!

Iron Age Village

The Iron Age of Britain began around 750 B.C.E. and lasted around 800 years. During this time, major developments took place in every aspect of human life, as can be seen here in this large-scale model depicting pioneering agricultural processes, a stone circle for religious rituals, and some large hillforts containing roundhouses. Remnants of these settlements are still visible in the landscape today – pretty impressive, given they were built over 2,000 years ago!

ASSASSINATION OF JULIUS CAESAR, 44 B.C.E.

The Roman statesman Gaius Julius Caesar led the Roman invasion of Britain and is seen as one of the greatest military commanders in history. After his military career, Caesar looked back at the Roman Republic and decided that the government had become corrupt and powerless, and should be replaced. He led his army back into Rome and set himself as dictator. Caesar did many great things while in power, including starting a police force and creating the Julian calendar (which we still use today). Things didn't go well for Caesar, though. On the Ides of March (the 15th) in 44 B.C.E., he was attacked by as many as 60 senators wanting freedom from his reign and was stabbed 23 times. Caesar's death led to five civil wars and ultimately the creation of the Roman Empire.

ROMAN LAUREL WREATH

The laurel wreath might be associated with the Romans, but it's actually been in use since ancient Greek times. Throughout history, the laurel wreath has been a symbol of victory – whether in military or in sport. In some countries, the laurel wreath signifies academic achievement, perhaps getting a degree or finishing a course. This laurel wreath can be completed by anyone, though, as a celebration of becoming an expert builder! I've used different colours in my wreath, but you can use whatever you like. And if the wreath is too big or small to wear, simply take out one set of the tree elements or use a shorter string.

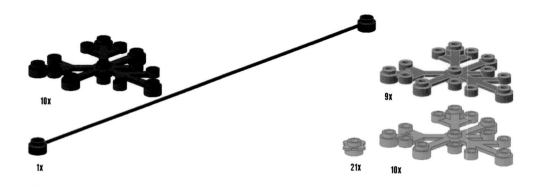

10x

1x

9x

21x   10x

1

2

3

4

5

6

7

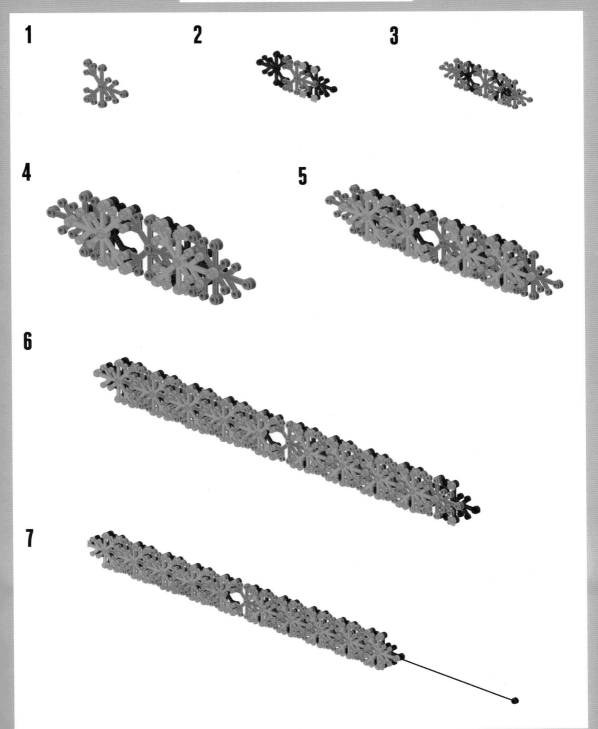

BURIAL OF POMPEII, 79 C.E.

Much of what we know about the Romans comes from documented history – books and scrolls. However, we are also lucky enough to have some amazing archaeological finds too – especially Pompeii! Situated near modern-day Naples in Italy, Pompeii was a thriving town in Roman times until disaster struck. A nearby volcano, Mount Vesuvius, suddenly erupted in 79 C.E. Rather than spewing out molten rock, this eruption ejected millions of tons of ash into the atmosphere. The ash rained down on the people of Pompeii, covering everything and sealing it in for future scientists to uncover. The amazingly well-preserved remains of houses, streets and even people have led to many discoveries about Roman life.

CORONATION OF CHARLEMAGNE, 800

After the fall of the Roman Empire, much of Europe broke apart into a series of small kingdoms. One of the largest of these was the Kingdom of the Franks, and its most celebrated leader was Charlemagne. Born around 745, he laid the foundations for modern Germany and France. Involved in battles throughout most of his life, he became king of Italy and the first Holy Roman Emperor. He also pushed the empire into parts of modern Spain and Austria, and beyond. Today, he is considered to be the father of the French and German royal families. It's not for nothing that he's known as the Father of Europe.

VIKING INVASIONS

The Vikings came from all over Scandinavia – Denmark, Sweden, Norway and even Iceland and the Faroe Islands. What they all have in common, though, is their amazing seafaring skills. From the eighth to the eleventh centuries, Vikings traded across the North Sea in longboats. Today, it's believed that they were such good mariners that they were able to cross the Atlantic to North America. Sadly, Vikings have been characterised as the bad guys for many years. Modern research paints a very different picture, though. There is no evidence they ever wore horned helmets, for instance. And a thirteenth-century writer detailed how good their personal hygiene was – they combed their hair and washed regularly, up to once a week!

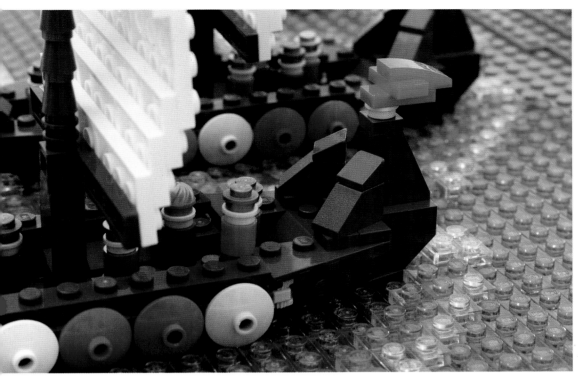

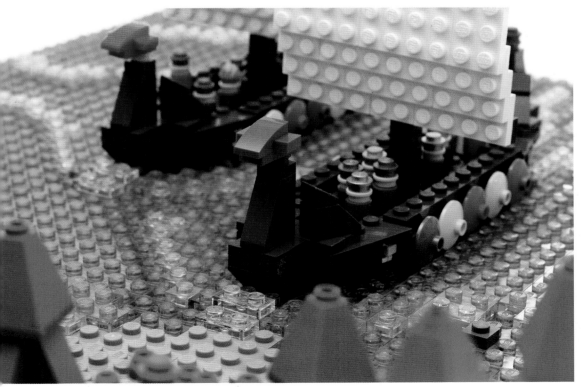

VIKING SHIELD

Viking shields were usually made of a strong wood – archaeologists have recovered shields made of fir, alder and poplar. Having a strong shield was important, as it might have been the only protection a Viking warrior had against a spear or an axe. These wood types are also light, which is important when you have to carry your shield with you. To enhance its protection, Vikings would often add leather or occasionally an iron rim to the shield. This LEGO® model uses the technique of 'SNOT' (Studs Not On Top). Four sides of the shield are built so that the studs point outwards, resulting in a much smoother curve.

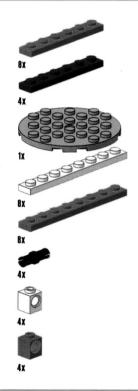

8x

4x

1x

8x

8x

4x

4x

4x

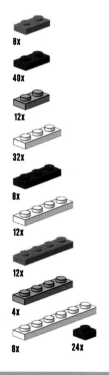

8x

40x

12x

32x

8x

12x

12x

4x

8x

24x

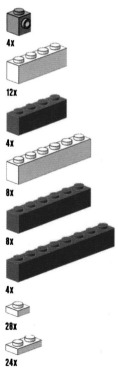

4x

12x

4x

8x

8x

4x

28x

24x

4x

16x

20x

4x

12x

4x

4x

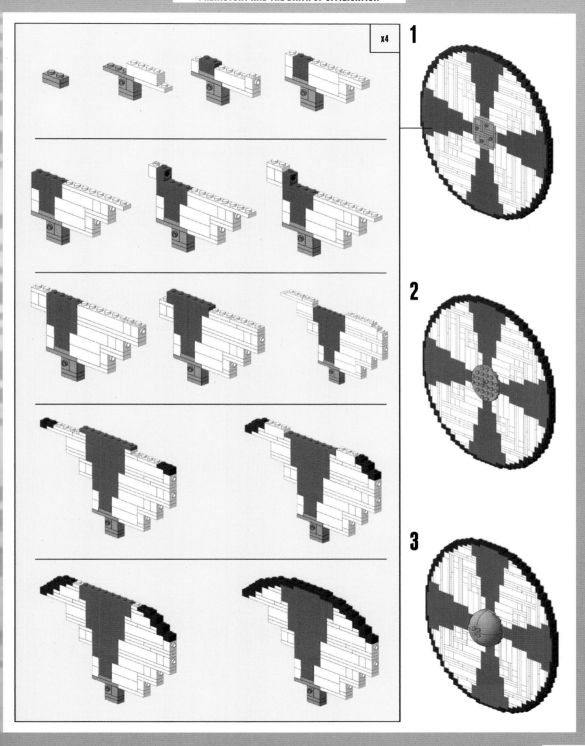

THE BATTLE OF HASTINGS, 1066

Ask anyone in the United Kingdom to name one ancient battle and a particular one will almost always pop up. The Battle of Hastings in 1066 is written into the memory of the English. It was the last stand of the Anglo-Saxons who inhabited England at the time against the invading Norman army from France. After Edward the Confessor died, there was a fight for the throne. The Anglo-Saxon King Harold was given the crown, but it didn't come easy! Soon after the coronation, he marched his army north to fight off an invasion by the Norwegian king. That battle won, he had to suddenly march back south to fight off another invasion. 17,000 people took to the fields outside the port of Hastings. Late in the battle, an arrow shot straight to the eye killed Harold, leading to the collapse of the Saxon army and the coronation of William the Conqueror.

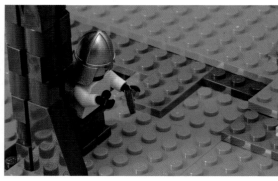

Genghis Khan's Mongol Empire, 1206–1227

It's almost certain that Genghis Khan's Mongol 'hordes' spent their time in yurts. Herodotus first mentioned this traditional tent-like building around 450 B.C.E. The round structure has a wooden skeleton underneath a felt cover. The weight of the exterior covering balances the natural tendency of the wood to expand, keeping everything in place. When it's time to move on, the building can be disassembled and packed up so the parts can be easily carried. Yurts are still in use today, both in Asia and the West. Western yurts, though, tend to be more stationary.

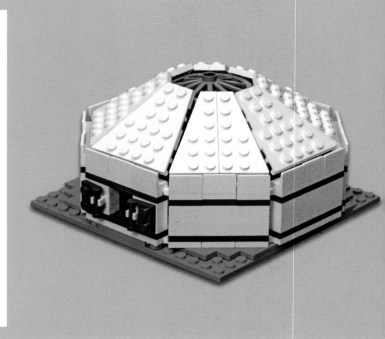

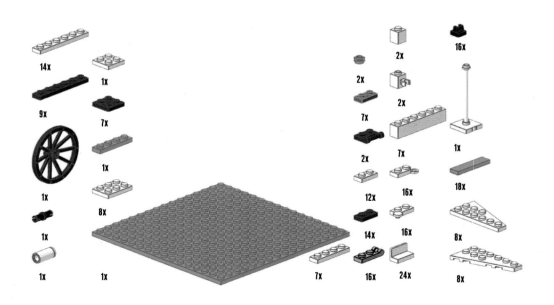

1

2

3

4

5

6

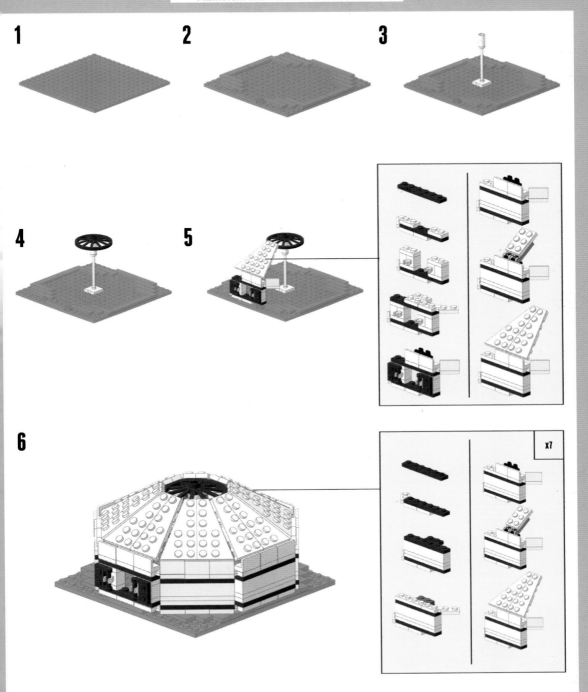

x7

EARLY NAVIGATION

The sextant was a major move forwards in the navigation of the seas – so much so that it's still used today. This highly sensitive instrument can be used to calculate both the longitude and latitude of your ship, placing it exactly on the globe. This LEGO® model is quite complex in itself, though it does work (to a degree!). It uses a technique common among LEGO fans – that is, using a 'flex tube' to create a subtle curve and then attaching 'plates with clip' to it at regular intervals. It's a clever technique that creates a nice shape.

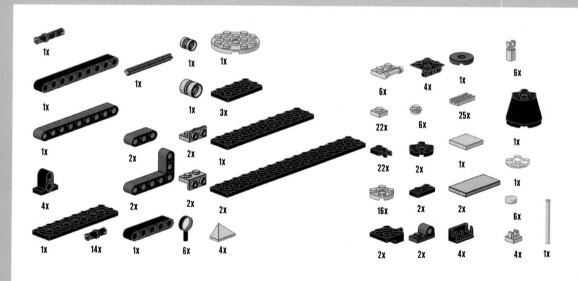

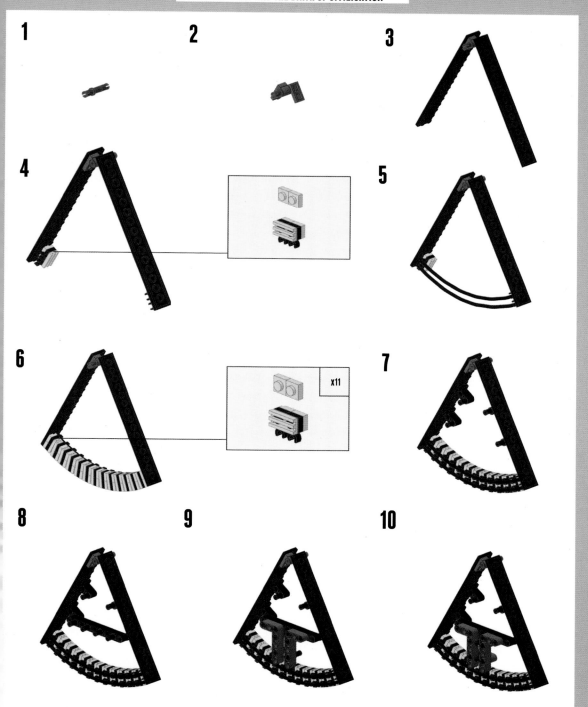

11

12

13

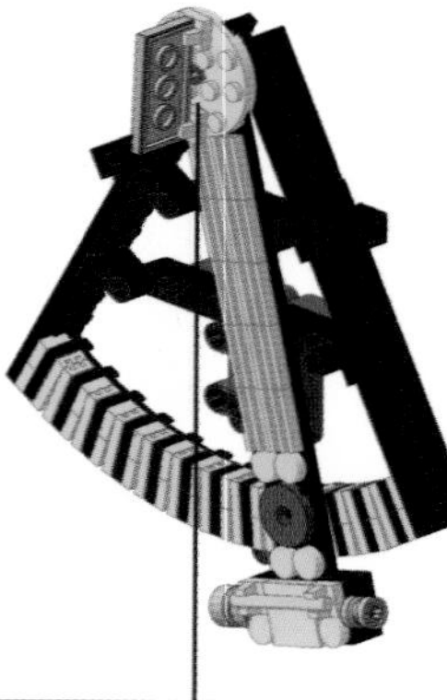

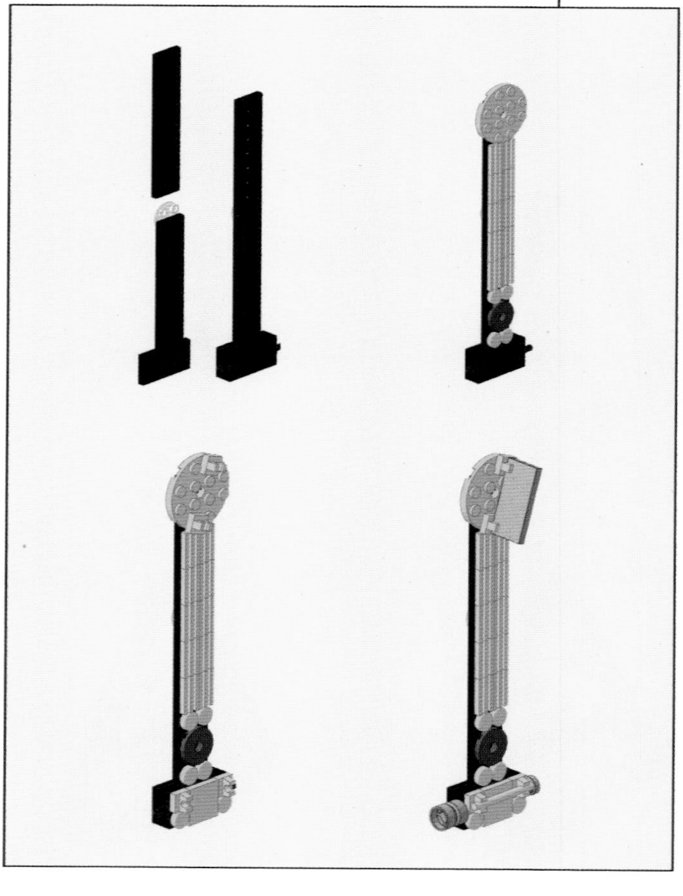

14

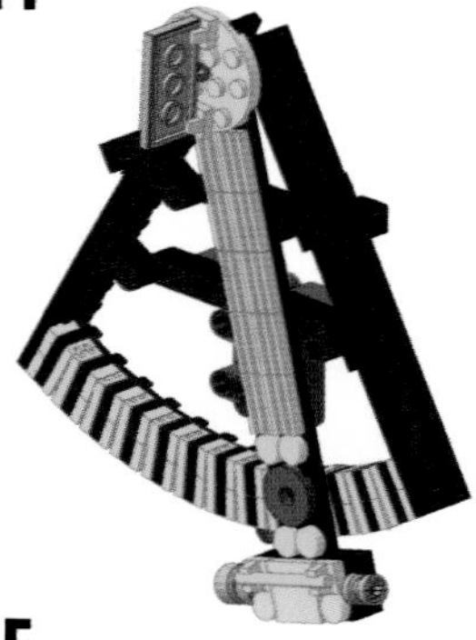

15

16

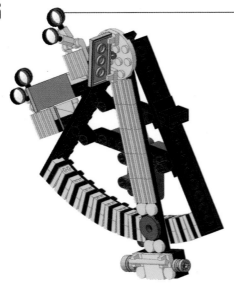

17

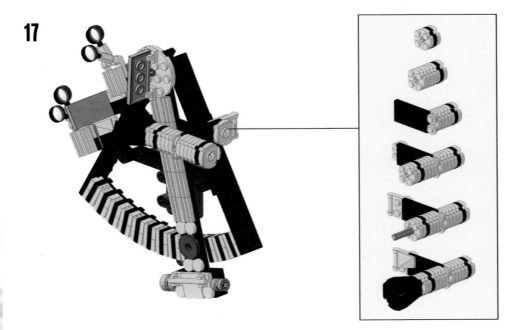

RENAISSANCE AND THE AGE OF EMPIRE

INVENTION OF THE GUTENBERG PRINTING PRESS, 1436

Before the invention of the Gutenberg Printing Press, books were expensive. Whereas people in East Asia were pressing books page by page as a block, everyone else was hand copying them. Gutenberg's press enabled the page to be set out, letter by letter, very quickly. A printing press could produce 3,600 pages a day. Cheap and easily available printed books led to a dramatic rise in literacy rates and helped to fuel the Industrial Revolution.

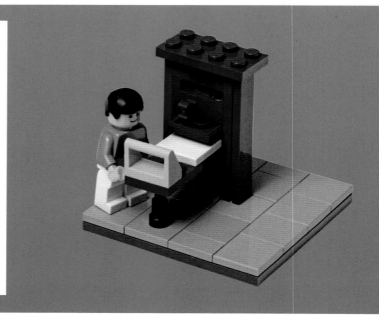

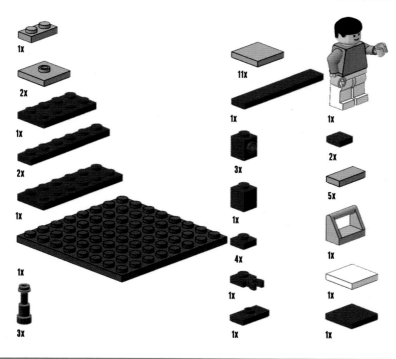

1x

2x

1x

2x

1x

1x

3x

11x

1x

3x

1x

4x

1x

1x

1x

2x

5x

1x

1x

1x

1

2

3

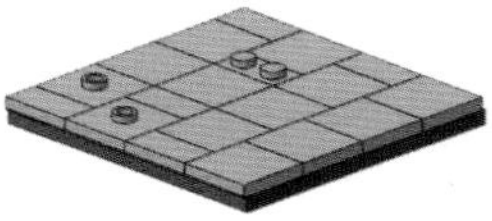

4

5

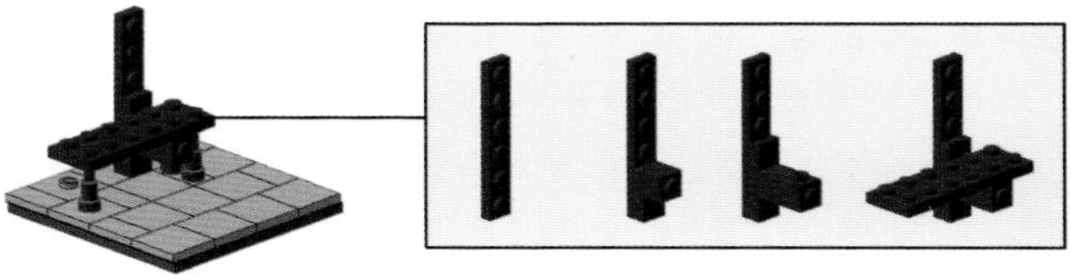

6

7

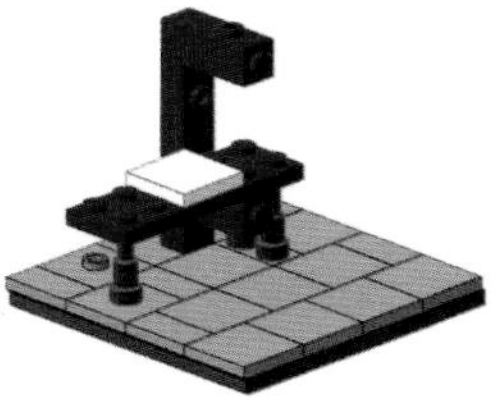

8

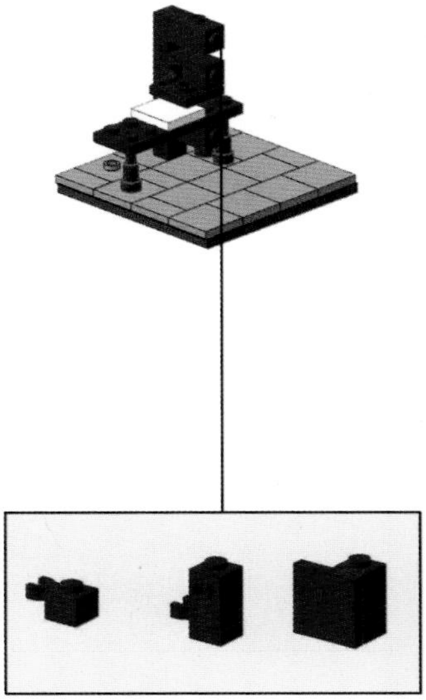

9

10

Leonardo da Vinci's Flying Machine, 1485

It might have taken until the twentieth century for human-powered flight to become a reality in everyday life, but that doesn't mean the idea is new! Leonardo da Vinci is famous for being both a painter and an inventor. His idea for a flying machine dates back to the fifteenth century. Sadly, we know now that although his ideas were logical, this machine could never have been built in his time. The wooden materials he would have used were far too heavy for a design such as this. But da Vinci did blaze the trail for inventors all around the world – and we use many of his other designs to this day.

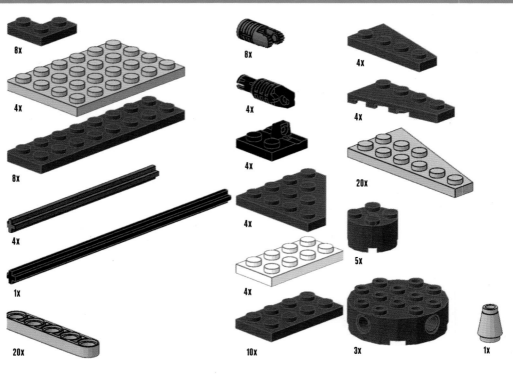

8x

4x

8x

4x

1x

20x

8x

4x

4x

4x

4x

20x

4x

5x

10x

3x

4x

4x

1x

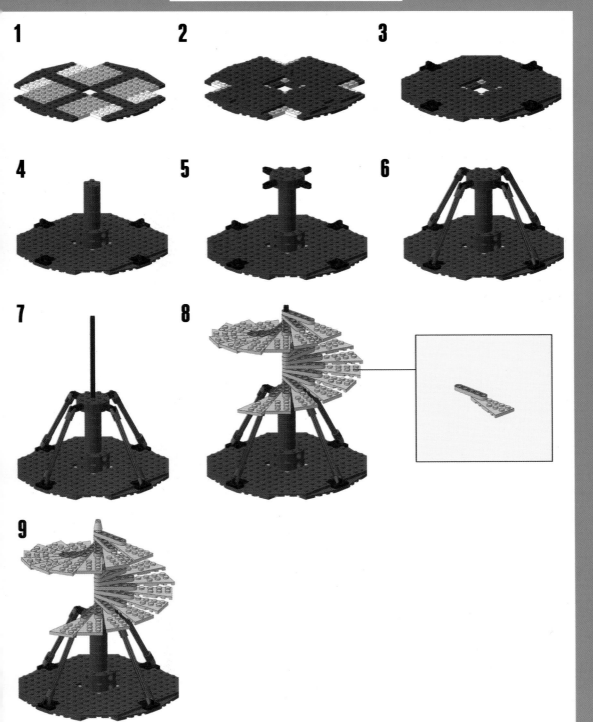

1

2

3

4

5

6

7

8

9

MICHELANGELO PAINTS THE SISTINE CHAPEL CEILING, 1508–1512

It took Michelangelo four years to paint the ceiling of the Sistine Chapel, located in the heart of the Vatican in Rome, but if you are ever lucky enough to visit it, you'll realise why. This work is celebrated as one of the finest pieces of Renaissance art. Measuring 40 metres long by 13 metres wide (131.5ft x 42.5ft), the painting is a monumental achievement, and is now one of the world's most visited tourist attractions, with over five million people visiting each year.

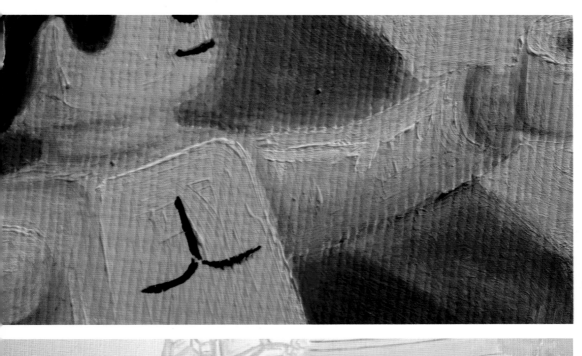

MICHELANGELO'S PALETTE

If you're about to create a masterpiece painting, then you'll need a palette to mix up your colours. This LEGO® design is actually much more complex than it looks. To achieve the illusion of smooth convex and concave curves, I've used a combination of slopes, inverted slopes and curved slopes. Each of these parts needs to be placed the correct way, so the palette is made of three main sections — going up, down and right. There's also a neat little trick in the middle to create the thumbhole. Using two 'headlight' bricks, I've reversed the direction of the studs and mounted an arch piece upside down.

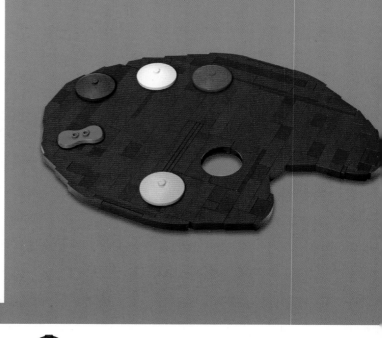

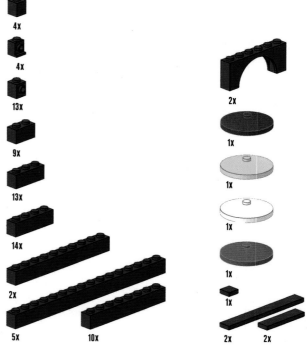

1x
3x
5x
2x
3x
5x
4x
3x
4x
7x
1x
2x
5x
4x
10x
2x
1x

4x
4x
13x
9x
13x
14x
2x
5x
10x

2x
1x
1x
1x
1x
1x
2x
2x

1

2

3

4

5

6

7

8

9

10

11

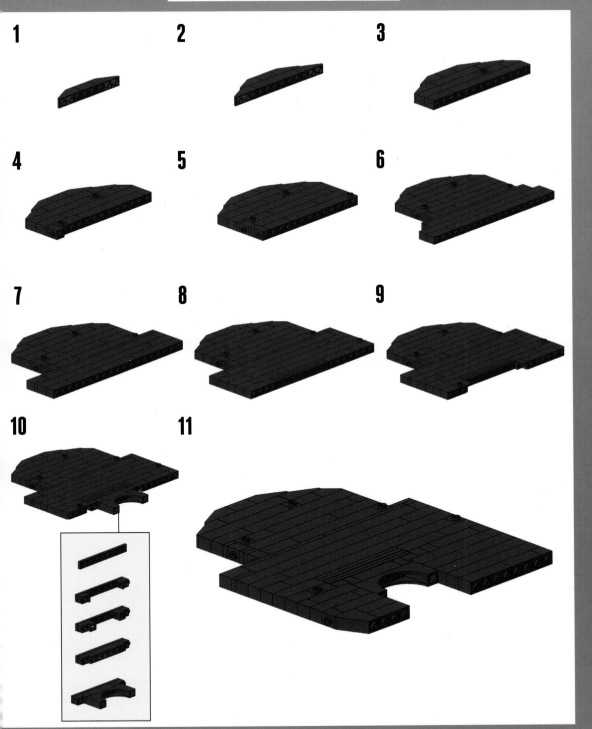

12

13

14

15

16

17

18

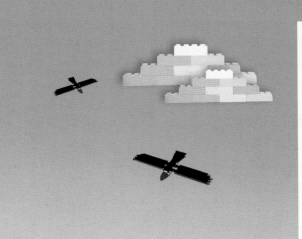

SPANISH CONQUEST OF AZTEC EMPIRE, 1521

Just as the Dutch and then the British invaded what is modern-day New England in the 1500s, the Spanish invaded what is now Mexico. Christopher Columbus's expeditions uncovered new land rich with wildlife, people and of course precious metals. Conquering new land was a way to get rich and grow the empire. Cortés led the expedition in 1519, and although many of his men had no previous combat experience, it was only two years later that the Aztec capital of Tenochtitlan was seized. In contrast, the entire conquest of the Yucatán Peninsula took almost 170 years. In fact, were it not for disease and epidemics (which killed around 75 percent of the native people), the process would have taken much, much longer.

COPERNICUS DISCOVERS HELIOCENTRISM, 1543

Before Copernicus, everyone assumed that the Earth was at the centre of the universe. But in 1543, the publication of his book, *On the Revolutions of the Celestial Spheres*, changed all that. That book put the sun at the centre of the known universe, with planets orbiting around it. Although we now know that's not true, the idea that Earth wasn't at the centre of everything contributed to the Scientific Revolution. Our model is a working representation of this – an orrery. In the model, you can clearly see how the Earth orbits the sun and the moon orbits the Earth.

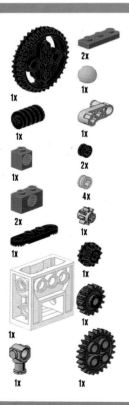

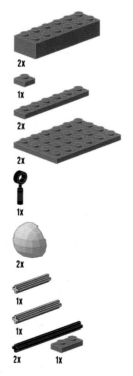

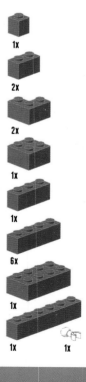

1

2

3

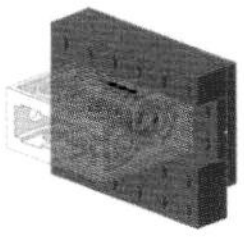

4

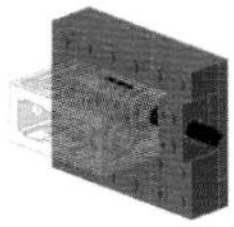

5

6

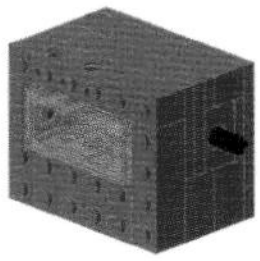

7

8

9

10

11

12

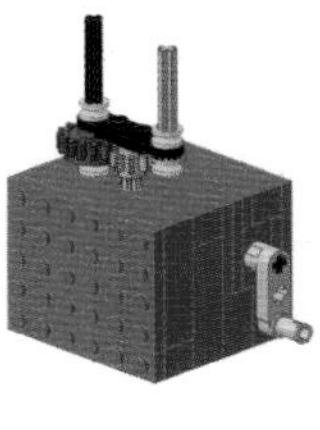

13

14

15

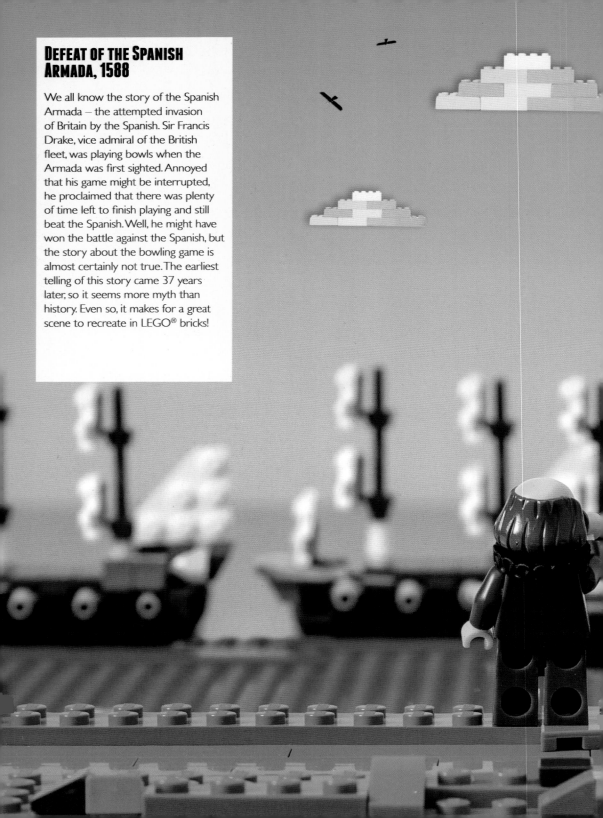

DEFEAT OF THE SPANISH ARMADA, 1588

We all know the story of the Spanish Armada – the attempted invasion of Britain by the Spanish. Sir Francis Drake, vice admiral of the British fleet, was playing bowls when the Armada was first sighted. Annoyed that his game might be interrupted, he proclaimed that there was plenty of time left to finish playing and still beat the Spanish. Well, he might have won the battle against the Spanish, but the story about the bowling game is almost certainly not true. The earliest telling of this story came 37 years later, so it seems more myth than history. Even so, it makes for a great scene to recreate in LEGO® bricks!

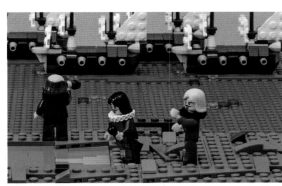

SIR FRANCIS DRAKE'S
GOLDEN HIND

Queen Elizabeth I's ships were also famous for their great adventures exploring the stormy seas. This miniature galleon is based on the *Golden Hind*, sailed by Sir Francis Drake – her favourite explorer – between 1577 and 1580 around the coast of South America. Sir Francis was also given special permission to attack and plunder any Spanish vessels that crossed his path, resulting in his knighthood and the Queen's acquisition of nearly £160,000!

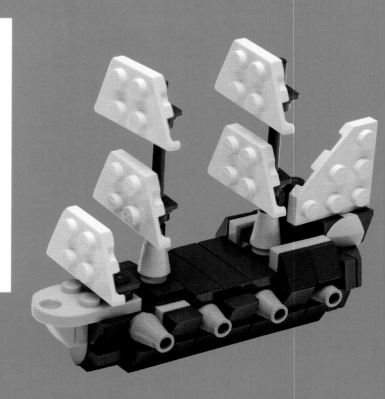

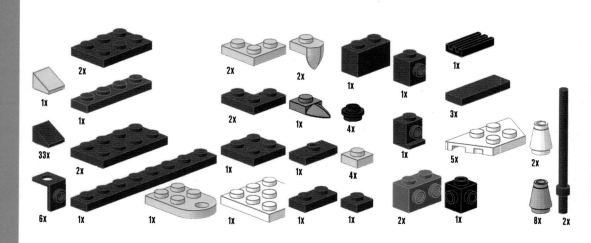

1

2

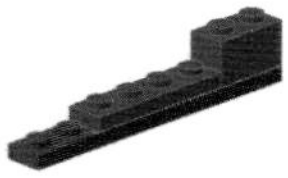

3

4

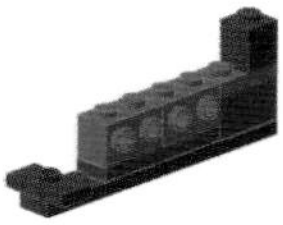

5

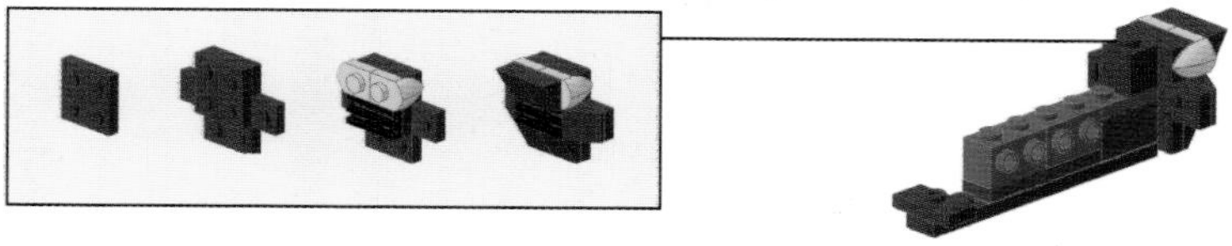

6

7

8

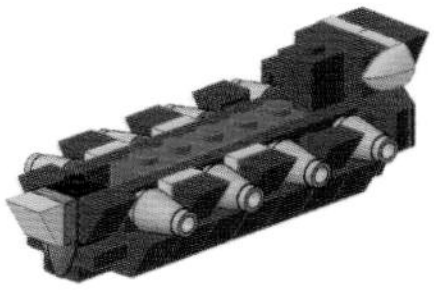

9

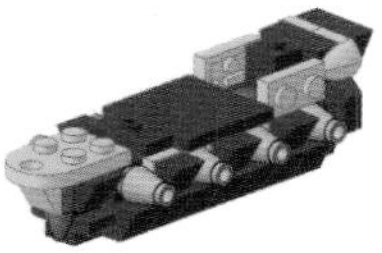

10

11

12

13

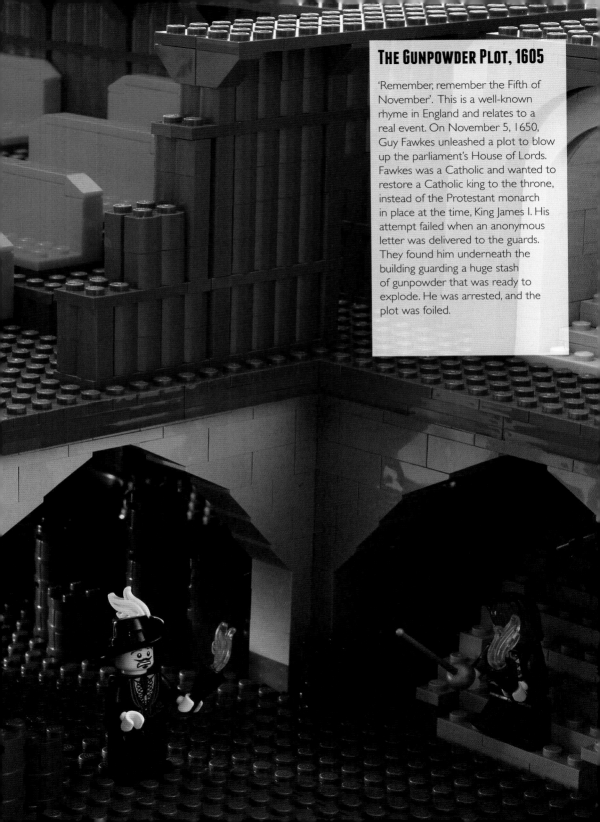

THE GUNPOWDER PLOT, 1605

'Remember, remember the Fifth of November'. This is a well-known rhyme in England and relates to a real event. On November 5, 1650, Guy Fawkes unleashed a plot to blow up the parliament's House of Lords. Fawkes was a Catholic and wanted to restore a Catholic king to the throne, instead of the Protestant monarch in place at the time, King James I. His attempt failed when an anonymous letter was delivered to the guards. They found him underneath the building guarding a huge stash of gunpowder that was ready to explode. He was arrested, and the plot was foiled.

Every year since then, celebrations have been held on November 5 across the United Kingdom. An effigy of Guy Fawkes ('the 'Guy') is burned on a bonfire and fireworks are launched so that we never forget 'gunpowder, treason and plot'.

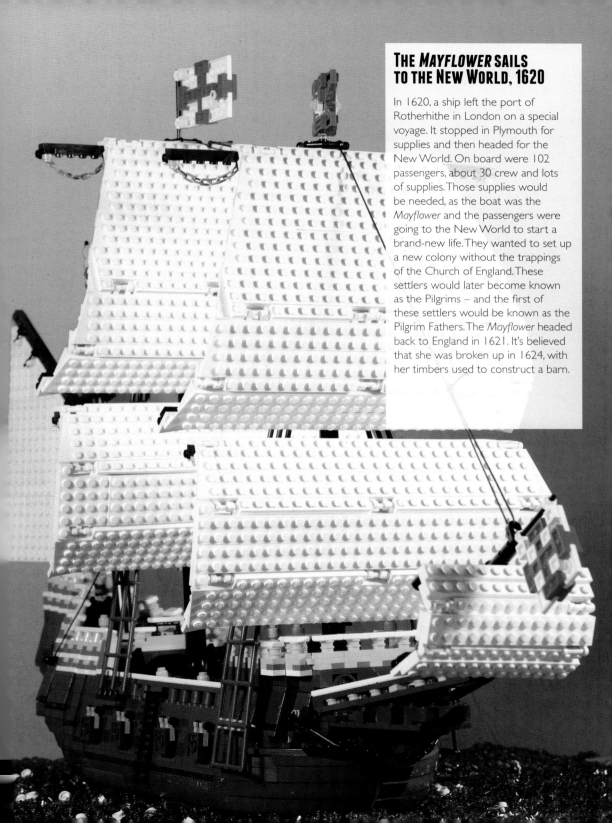

THE *MAYFLOWER* SAILS TO THE NEW WORLD, 1620

In 1620, a ship left the port of Rotherhithe in London on a special voyage. It stopped in Plymouth for supplies and then headed for the New World. On board were 102 passengers, about 30 crew and lots of supplies. Those supplies would be needed, as the boat was the *Mayflower* and the passengers were going to the New World to start a brand-new life. They wanted to set up a new colony without the trappings of the Church of England. These settlers would later become known as the Pilgrims – and the first of these settlers would be known as the Pilgrim Fathers. The *Mayflower* headed back to England in 1621. It's believed that she was broken up in 1624, with her timbers used to construct a barn.

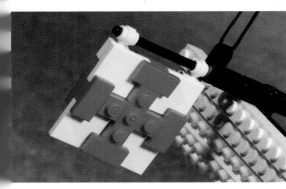
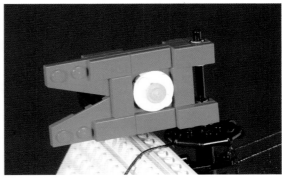

THE GREAT FIRE OF LONDON, 1666

In 1666, a great fire ravaged London. Starting on Sunday night, on September 2, it erupted in a bakery on Pudding Lane. This wasn't that uncommon, and the standard practice to fight fires at the time was to demolish the buildings around the one on fire. That way, the fire could be stopped. This time, though, the neighbours objected to having their homes knocked down, so the Lord Mayor was called to make a decision. By the time he did, the fire had already taken hold. Four days later, more than 13,000 homes, almost 100 churches, and St. Paul's Cathedral had been destroyed.

LONDON TOWNHOUSE

Recreating the fire of London in LEGO® bricks is no mean feat! With so many houses crammed into central London, there was only one way to represent the disaster. The houses in our scene – such as this one – are very small; only a few bricks wide. That means we can fit lots of buildings into a very small space. Building the houses sideways means we can use the plates' thickness instead of a brick, giving much more detail.

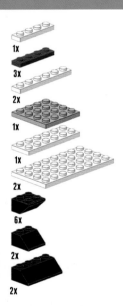

1x
3x
2x
1x
1x
2x
6x
2x
2x

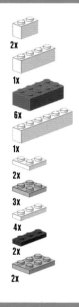

2x
1x
6x
1x
2x
3x
4x
2x
2x

1x
2x
4x
1x
1x
3x
7x
6x
1x
1x

1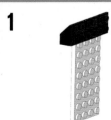

2

3

4

5

6

7

8

9

10

11

12

13

14

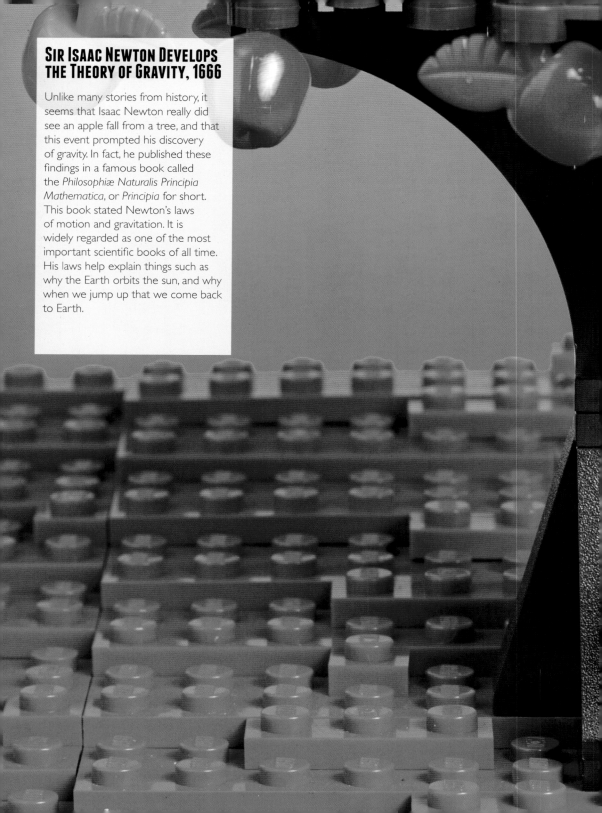

SIR ISAAC NEWTON DEVELOPS THE THEORY OF GRAVITY, 1666

Unlike many stories from history, it seems that Isaac Newton really did see an apple fall from a tree, and that this event prompted his discovery of gravity. In fact, he published these findings in a famous book called the *Philosophiæ Naturalis Principia Mathematica*, or *Principia* for short. This book stated Newton's laws of motion and gravitation. It is widely regarded as one of the most important scientific books of all time. His laws help explain things such as why the Earth orbits the sun, and why when we jump up that we come back to Earth.

Apple Drop, 1666

The drop of an apple inspired one of the most important scientific theories ever. This model of Newton's apple is a good example of how to make a curved surface with square LEGO® bricks. Although I've used four dome pieces to create the top of the apple, there isn't a part that exists that would work for the bottom. Instead, I've based my apple on a round plate, then used square 'inverted slopes' on each side. On their own, they probably wouldn't look very lifelike, but when put in between the curved plates, the eye is distracted – and a delicious and healthy snack emerges!

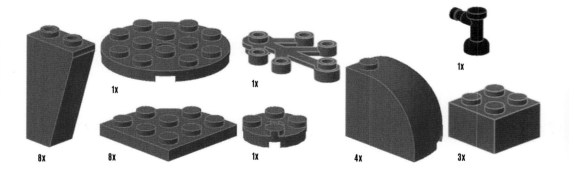

8x   1x   8x   1x   1x   4x   1x   3x

1

2

3

4

5

6

7

SALEM WITCH TRIALS, 1692

The Salem witch trials are some of America's darker moments, though this practice was by no means confined to the United States. In the seventeenth and eighteenth centuries, magic was thought to be real, and witches were feared. In Salem, a series of trials pronounced 26 men and women to be witches. Nineteen of them were hanged, and not actually burned at the stake – this is a popular myth.No one can be sure exactly why all this happened, but people's mass hysteria is now well understood. The trials are an example of crowd mentality – people behaving very differently in a crowd than when they think for themselves.

CAPTAIN COOK AND SIR JOSEPH BANKS EXPLORE THE SOUTH PACIFIC, 1772

Captain James Cook was a true explorer. On his first voyage, he sailed from England around Cape Horn and across the Pacific to New Zealand, and then onwards to Australia. When he and his crew arrived, they christened the area they explored Botany Bay after the unique specimens that the botanist on board, Sir Joseph Banks, had found. Banks was responsible for the classification of species such as the Eucalyptus and Acacia. Banks also advocated for the dubious practice of sending convicts there. It is his botanical studies that he is most remembered for, however, and we have recreated his pressed specimens using various LEGO® pieces. The leaves are actually dinosaur flippers!

BOSTON TEA PARTY, 1773

The Boston Tea Party was no party at all, but one of the defining moments in the struggle that led to the American Revolution. British citizens living in the United States had been asked to pay taxes. Unlike their fellow citizens living in Britain, however, they had no representation in parliament. 'No taxation without representation' became a rallying cry for the protestors. In 1773, it came to a head, and demonstrators dressed as Native Americans threw the entire tea cargo of three ships into Boston Harbor. This act escalated the conflict between Britain and the colonies, and eventually led to a revolution.

EAST INDIA TEA CRATE

This model tea crate is a very good example of the ratios of LEGO® bricks and plates. Five LEGO plates are the same height as four studs put sideways. So, by making this tea crate eight studs cubed, it's easier to connect the parts together securely at the fourth and eighth studs. Even so, to make a cube on all sides is quite difficult. You'll see that I've used brackets upside down to connect the bottom tiles. That's because these brackets allow for a special ½-plate offset, so I can attach the tiles on an odd number of the uprights.

2x

6x

4x

4x

4x

1x

16x

4x

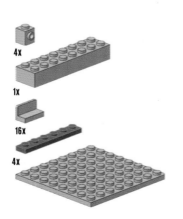

20x

10x

8x

8x

2x

4x

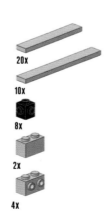

4x

8x

2x

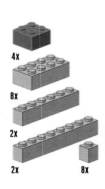

2x

8x

1

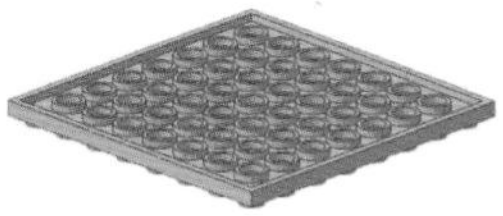

2

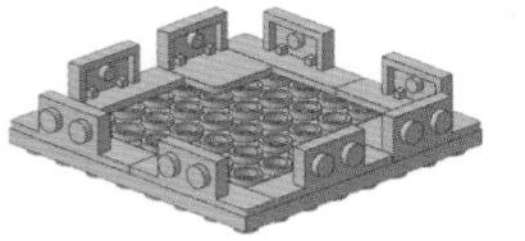

3

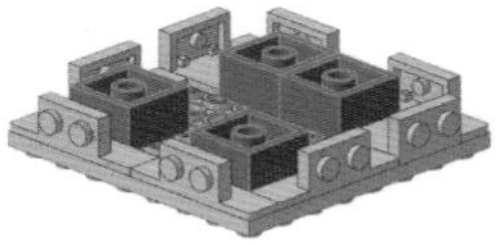

4

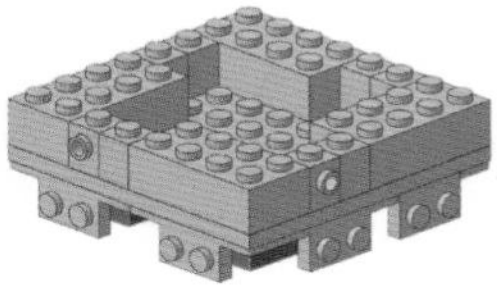

5

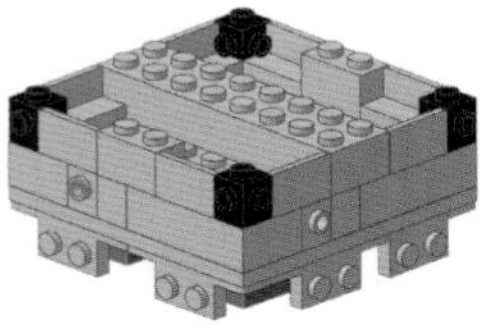

6

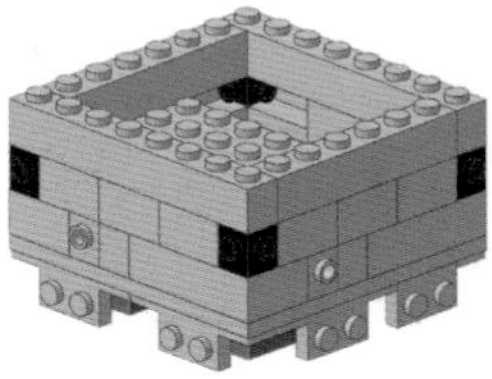

7

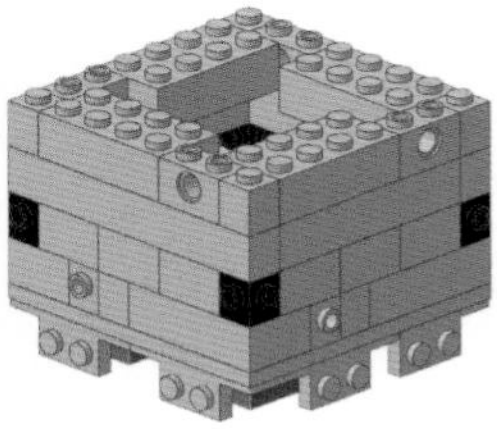

8

9

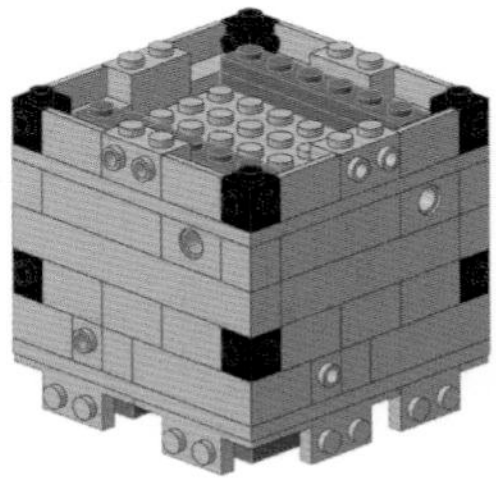

10

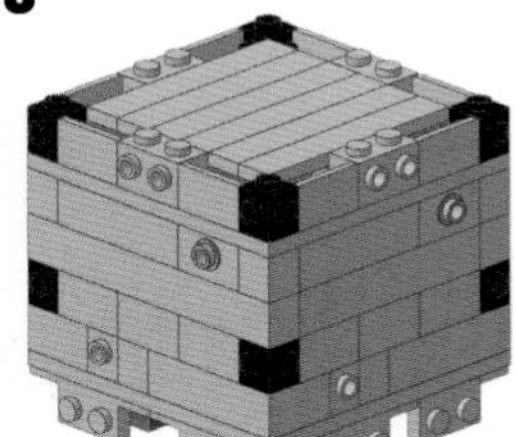

11

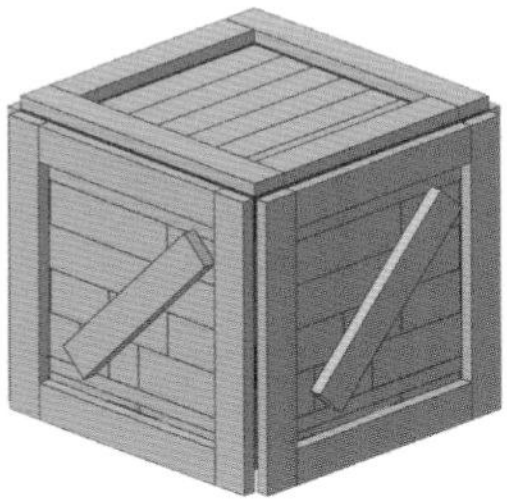

AMERICAN INDEPENDENCE, 1775–1783

The Declaration of Independence was written in 1776 during the Revolutionary War. It sought to ratify that the 13 colonies fighting the British were not separate entities, but rather would form a new nation – the United States of America. More than just that, it contained key statements that would form the backbone of the United States. 'All men are created equal' and 'certain unalienable rights' are phrases that will be recognisable to anyone in the Western world. Although the Declaration unified the American forces against the British, it was also ridiculed. And even though the Declaration pronounced that all men were equal, its author, Thomas Jefferson, was himself a prominent slave owner. Independence was finally achieved with the signing of the Treaty of Paris in September 1783.

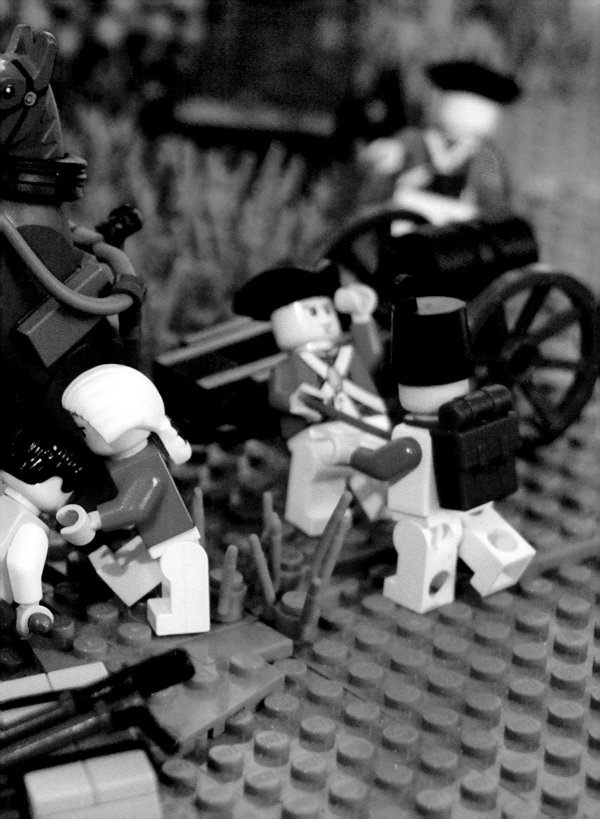

UNITED STATES CONSTITUTION, 1789

Following the Declaration of Independence and the end of the war in 1783, the United States of America created their Constitution, the official law of the nation, the enforcement of which is represented here by this gavel. Constitution judges use gavels to control a trial, and auctioneers use them to signal the final bid in a sale. Hitting a gavel against a hard surface makes a loud noise that signifies a deal is done. Although common in the United States and on pretty much every TV show, did you know that judges in the United Kingdom don't use gavels?

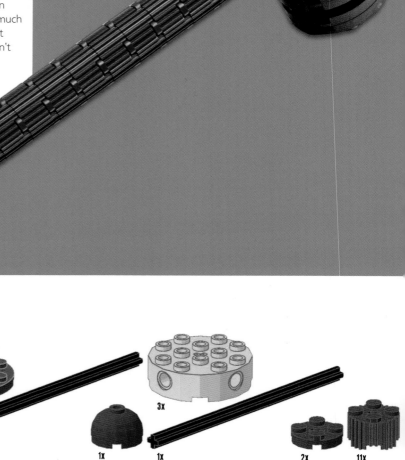

1x

2x

9x

1x

3x

1x

1x

2x

11x

1

2

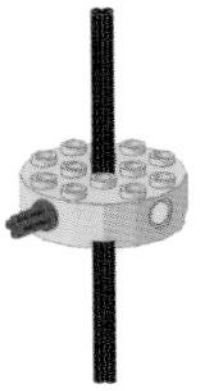

3

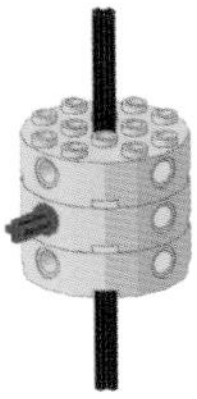

4

5

6

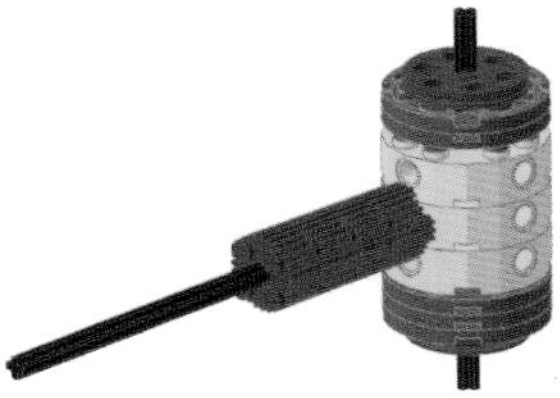

7

8

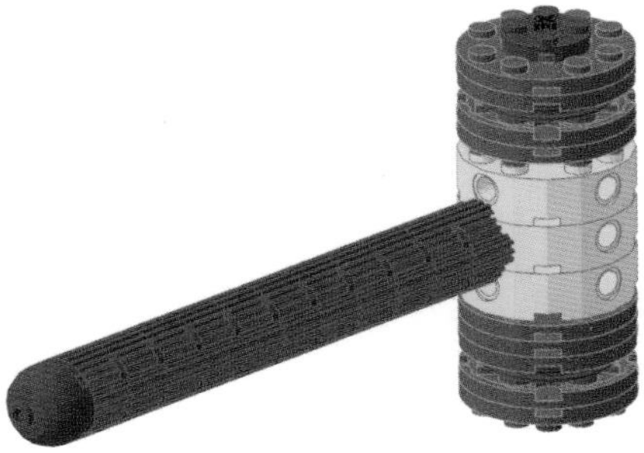

THE BIRTH OF THE INDUSTRIAL REVOLUTION, 1760–1820

The Industrial Revolution wasn't a single point in time, but rather over a relatively short period changed the way the world produced goods. Before the revolution, things were produced in small quantities at home or in workshops. The Industrial Revolution introduced factories, machinery and automation. Driven by water, steam and coal, the world changed rapidly. One such example is this iron bridge, built in a town in England, also called Ironbridge. This was the world's first arched bridge built out of cast iron, and is widely regarded as a symbol of the revolution.

MOZART COMPOSES
THE MAGIC FLUTE, 1791

The Magic Flute (or *Die Zauberflöte*) was one of the last operas Wolfgang Amadeus Mozart would write before his death. Throughout history, music has played an important part in human culture and storytelling. Many people now look at Mozart as one of the great classical composers. He started as a young child and was already composing by the age of five.

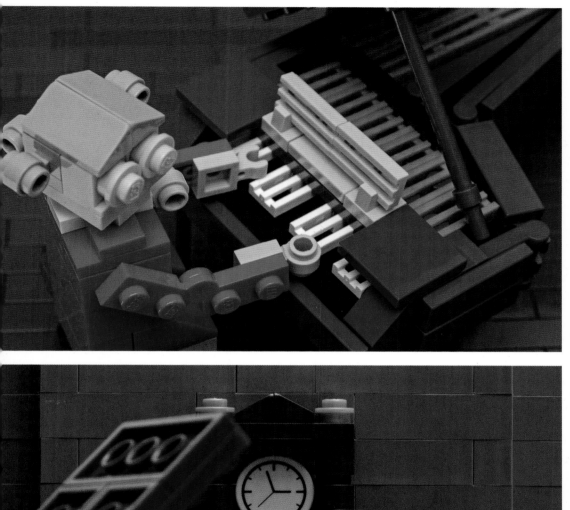

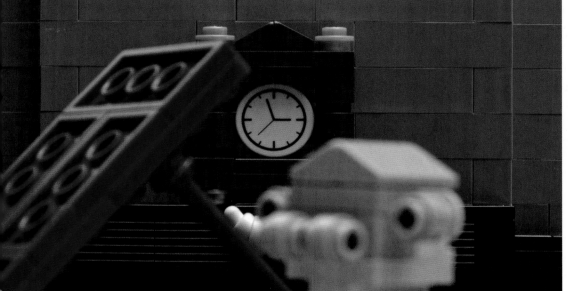

SMALLPOX VACCINE, 1798

In 1798, English scientist Edward Jenner developed the world's first vaccine to fight the terrible smallpox outbreak. Jenner noticed that dairymaids who had caught cowpox (a similar, but much less deadly virus) tended not to contract smallpox. He tested this theory by purposefully infecting an eight-year-old boy with cowpox and then smallpox. Risky, but it worked! Vaccination 'teaches' the body's immune system how to deal with a new type of attack. Once the body has learned how to defend itself against cowpox, it can more easily fight off smallpox. Because of this discovery, Jenner is said to have saved more lives than any other human.

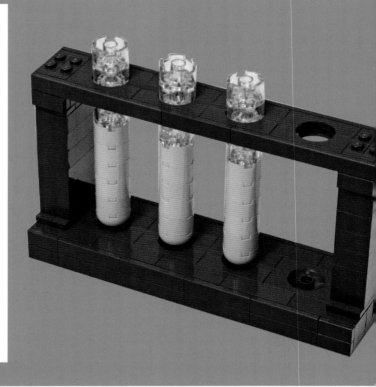

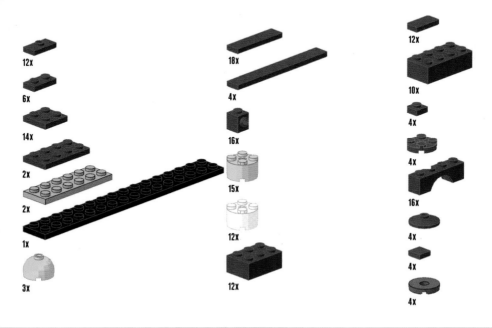

12x

6x

14x

2x

2x

1x

3x

18x

4x

16x

15x

12x

12x

12x

10x

4x

4x

16x

4x

4x

4x

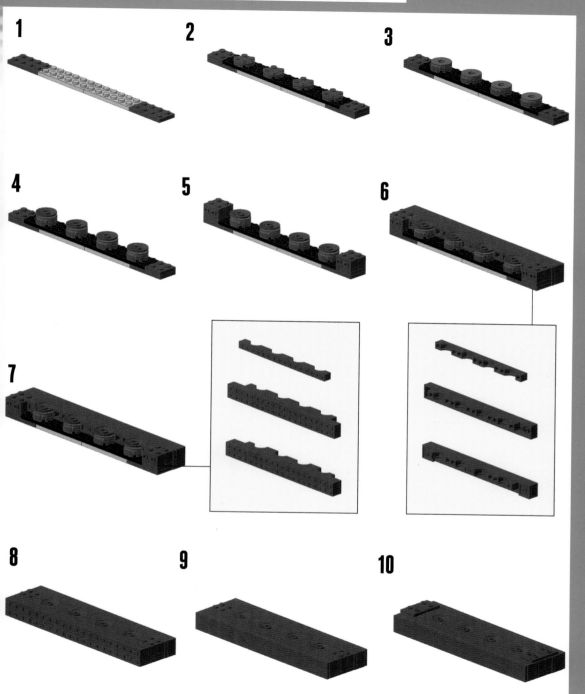

11

12

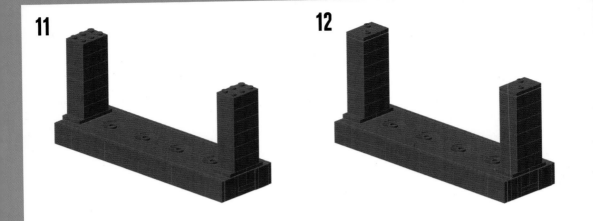

13

14

15

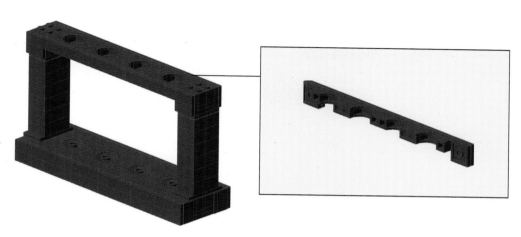

16

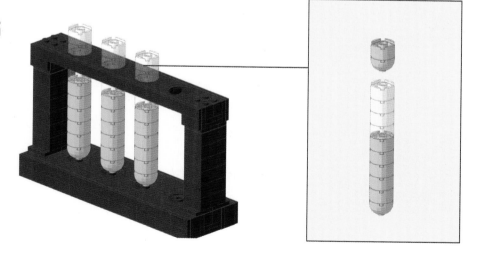

19th Century

The Battle of Trafalgar, 1805

The Battle of Trafalgar, which took place on October 21, 1805, saw 27 British ships fight against 33 French and Spanish ships as part of the Napoleonic Wars. Although it was a great victory for the British fleet, the battle is remembered for the death of just one person – Admiral Lord Nelson. Nelson was shot by a musket ball and died shortly afterwards. The scene of him lying next to his colleagues and friends is famous in naval history. On his deathbed, Nelson really did say, 'Kiss me, Hardy', which wasn't surprising considering that Captain Hardy was his closest friend.

NAVAL CANNON

Although LEGO® cannons exist, it would be cheating to use one of those! This brick-built cannon uses just a few parts to create an accurate shape of a cannon that would have been found on a ship during the Battle of Trafalgar. There are no parts in this model that face upwards; in fact, the two angled plates on the sides of the cannon do all the hard work – it's those parts that hold everything in place. But add wheel axles and the model becomes much sturdier. Probably not sturdy enough to fire a cannonball, though!

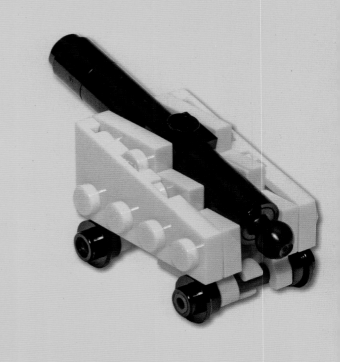

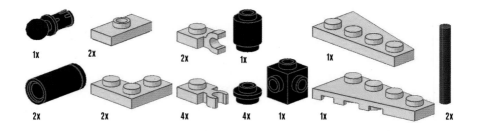

1x   2x   2x   1x   1x

2x   2x   4x   4x   1x   1x   2x

1

2

3

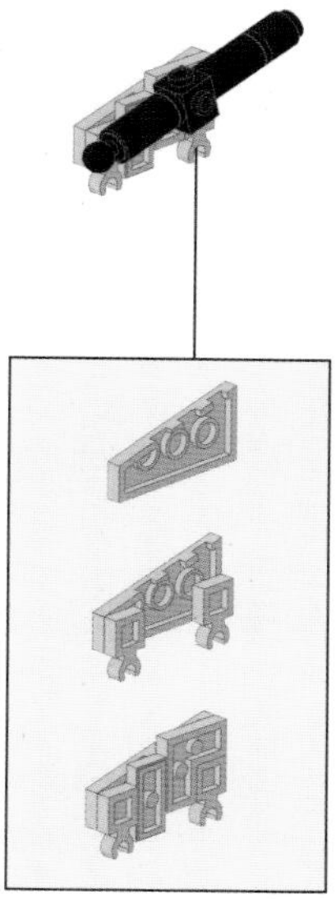

4

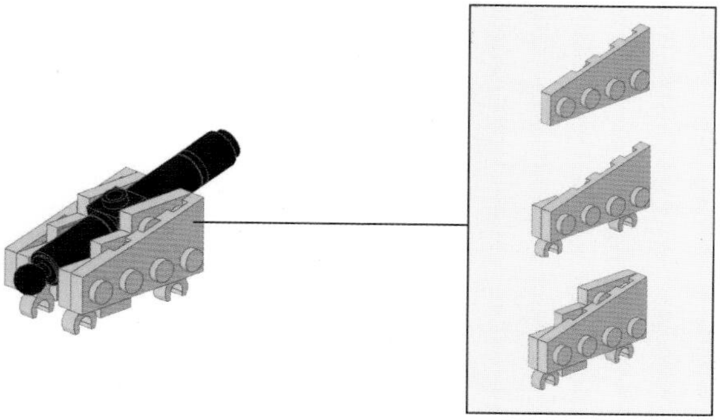

5

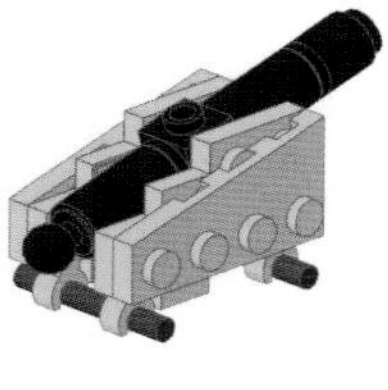

6

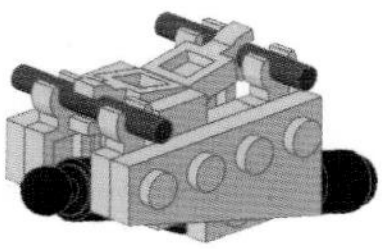

7

The Battle of Waterloo, 1815

The Battle of Waterloo was an important turning point in European history. The French army, under Napoleon, was beaten by the British army, led by the Duke of Wellington (yes, he of the Wellington boot!), combined with the Prussian army. Because of this battle, the first French empire came to an end. After the Battle of Waterloo, almost 40 years passed until the next war between countries in Europe (though it took more than 150 years to be immortalised in a song by the pop group ABBA!).

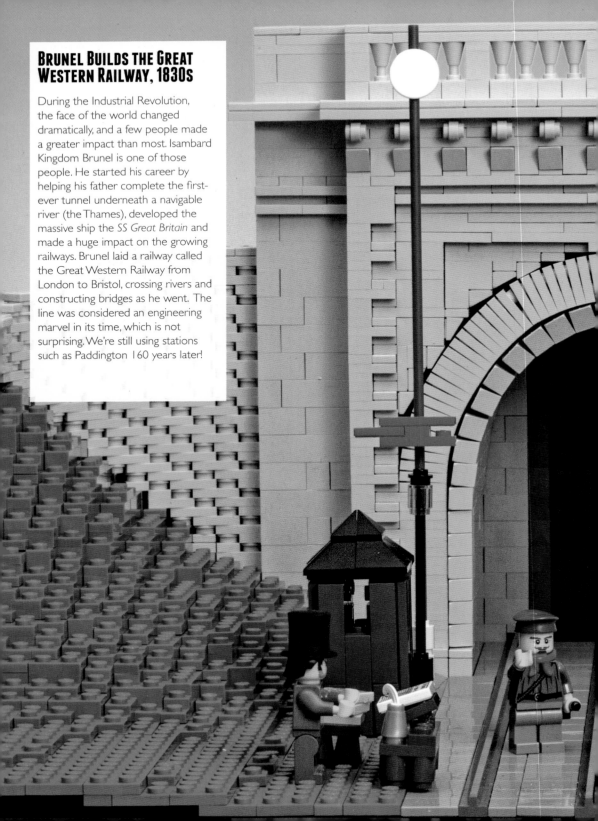

BRUNEL BUILDS THE GREAT WESTERN RAILWAY, 1830s

During the Industrial Revolution, the face of the world changed dramatically, and a few people made a greater impact than most. Isambard Kingdom Brunel is one of those people. He started his career by helping his father complete the first-ever tunnel underneath a navigable river (the Thames), developed the massive ship the *SS Great Britain* and made a huge impact on the growing railways. Brunel laid a railway called the Great Western Railway from London to Bristol, crossing rivers and constructing bridges as he went. The line was considered an engineering marvel in its time, which is not surprising. We're still using stations such as Paddington 160 years later!

THE GOLD RUSH, 1848

Surprisingly, the person who started the 1848 gold rush in California wasn't even looking for gold! James Wilson Marshall was in the process of constructing a lumber mill when he saw a shiny metal in a stream. After testing, it turned out to be gold. Soon after Marshall's discovery, around 300,000 people flocked to California, at that time a place with no major roads, towns, or even a proper government! There was no system of land ownership in place, so each prospector staked his or her own claim on a piece of land. It's now estimated that nearly 400 tons of gold were found in total, all retrieved by hand or very basic machinery such as this pickaxe.

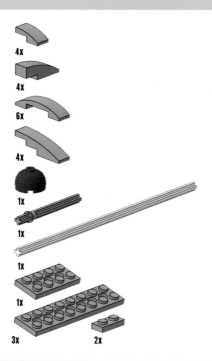

4x

4x

6x

4x

1x

1x

1x

1x

3x   2x

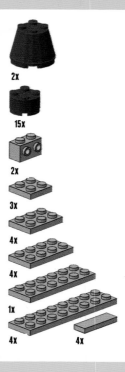

2x

15x

2x

3x

4x

4x

1x

4x   4x

1

2

3

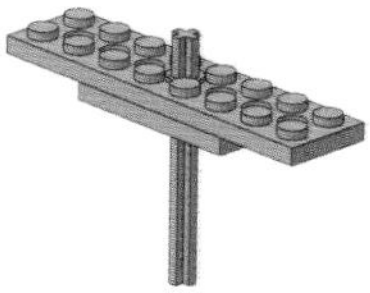

4

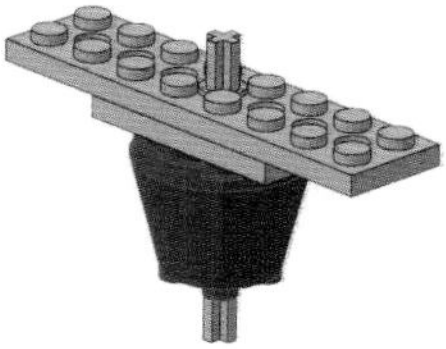

5

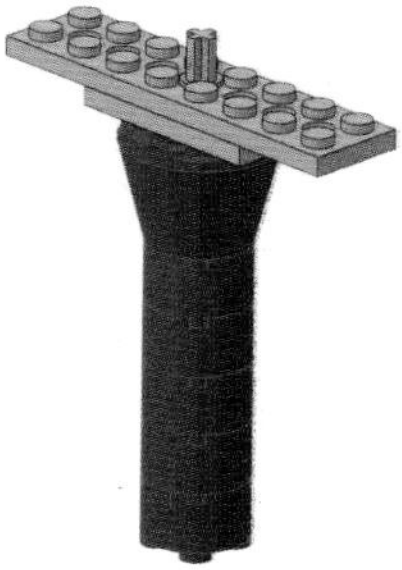

6

7

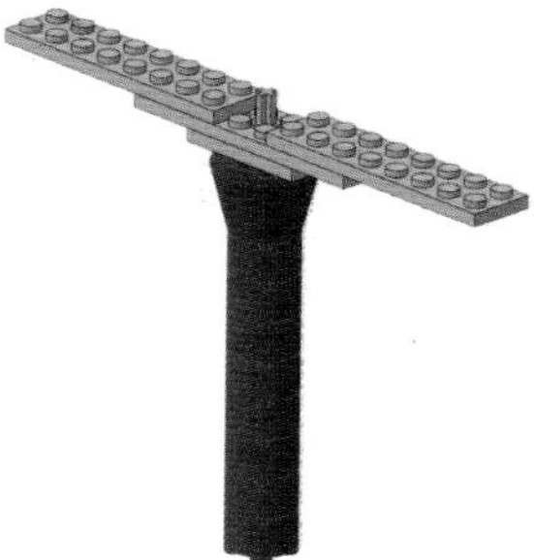

8

9

10

11

12

13

14

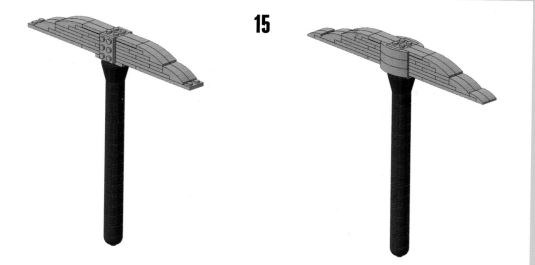

15

16

CHARLES DARWIN'S *ON THE ORIGIN OF SPECIES*, 1859

In 1859, Charles Darwin published one of the most important scientific papers known, *On the Origin of Species*. Darwin was one of the first people to discover that all living creatures have a common ancestry and that through the process of evolution and natural selection every individual species has evolved. It was during his time on the exploration ship the *Beagle* that he collected this vital data on evolution. Galápagos tortoises such as these are similar to ones on other islands but show slight variations, proving that they have adapted to their natural surroundings.

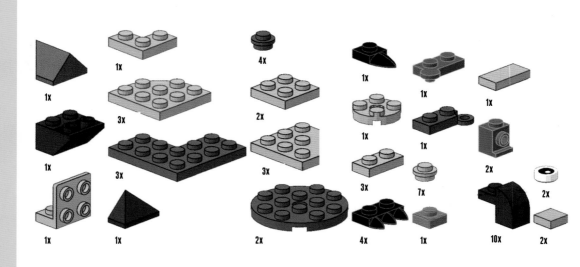

1

2

3

4

5

6

7

8

9

10

11

12

13

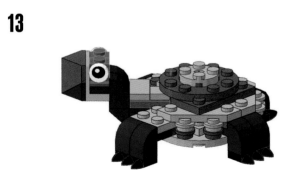

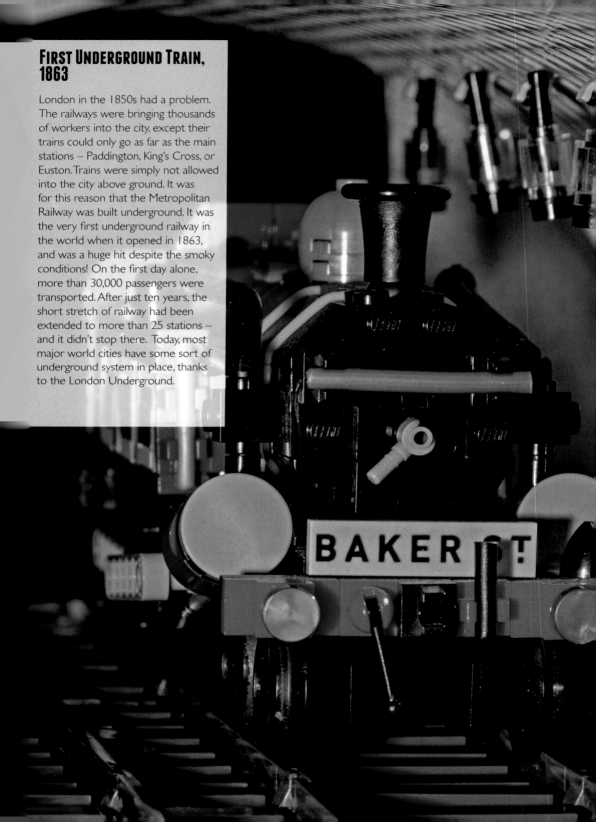

FIRST UNDERGROUND TRAIN, 1863

London in the 1850s had a problem. The railways were bringing thousands of workers into the city, except their trains could only go as far as the main stations – Paddington, King's Cross, or Euston. Trains were simply not allowed into the city above ground. It was for this reason that the Metropolitan Railway was built underground. It was the very first underground railway in the world when it opened in 1863, and was a huge hit despite the smoky conditions! On the first day alone, more than 30,000 passengers were transported. After just ten years, the short stretch of railway had been extended to more than 25 stations – and it didn't stop there. Today, most major world cities have some sort of underground system in place, thanks to the London Underground.

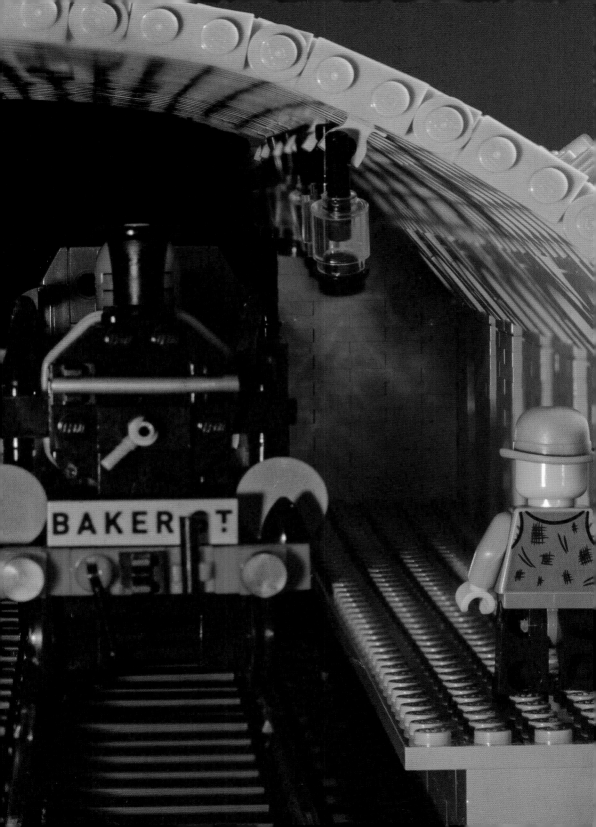

UNDERGROUND RAILROAD, MID-1800s

The Underground Railroad marks a dark period in American history, and has sadly nothing to do with tracks or trains. In the nineteenth century, the United States was split by one overriding fact: slavery was legal in the southern states and illegal in the northern ones. Many white people living throughout the United States thought the practice of slavery was wrong, so they helped slaves escape to the states where they could be free. The system of safe houses, special routes and meeting points was known as the Underground Railroad. It is estimated that 100,000 people escaped via this railroad.

THE AMERICAN CIVIL WAR AND ABOLITION OF SLAVERY, 1861–1865

In 1861, the newly formed United States was split by the issue of slavery. The government of the time wanted to make slavery illegal, but seven of the Deep South states were so against this that they decided to leave the United States entirely. These states called themselves the Confederate States of America, and a civil war broke out between the South and the North. The American Civil War lasted for four years and took the lives of 600,000 people, but eventually the Union in the north won, and slavery was abolished. Echoes of the Civil War still ripple through America, and opinions on the use of the Confederate flag vary widely.

20th MAINE AT

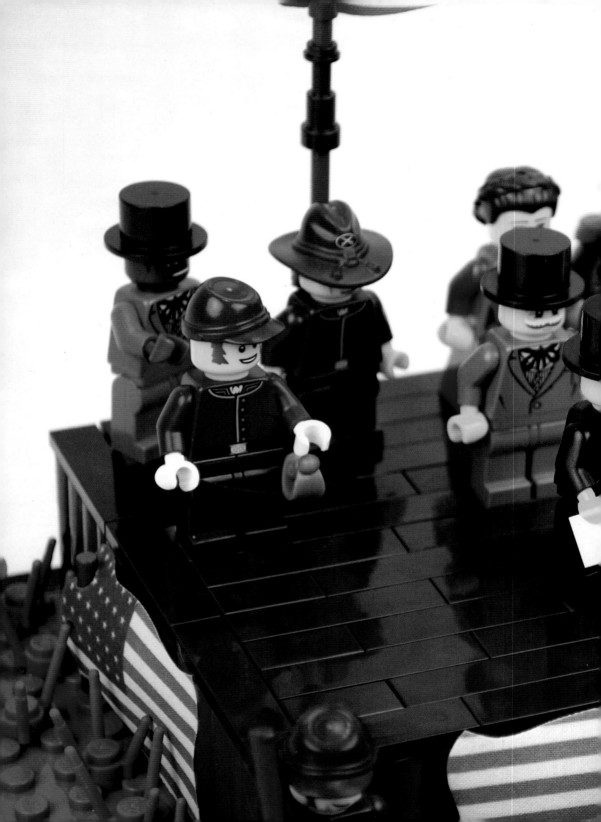

The Gettysburg Address, 1863

The Gettysburg Address is one of the most influential speeches of American history, but is also surprisingly short. This famous speech only took two minutes to deliver at the consecration of the Soldiers' National Cemetery on November 19, 1863, shortly after the Union soldiers defeated the Confederate Army at the Battle of Gettysburg – but scholars aren't exactly sure what was said! Although the famous 'Four score and seven years ago' start is undisputed, there is no actual evidence of the rest of the speech. Five different manuscripts have been found, all differing from the newspaper report of the time. Whatever the exact wording though, the outcome was the same. Lincoln's words have echoed throughout history and influenced numerous other struggles for equality.

INVENTION OF THE TELEPHONE, 1876

This might not look much like the telephone you're using today, but it's a pretty accurate model of the very earliest telephone invented by Alexander Graham Bell in 1876. The speaker talks into the black cone, which directs the sound waves from the voice into a central coil. The coil converts these vibrations into electrical signals that are sent along wires from the two screw terminals at the end. So, what were the first words ever spoken on this device? 'Watson, come here. I want to see you'.

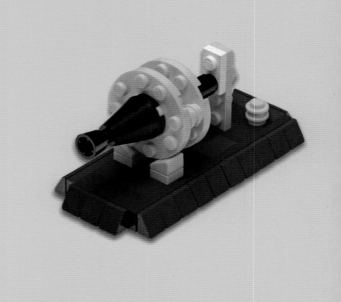

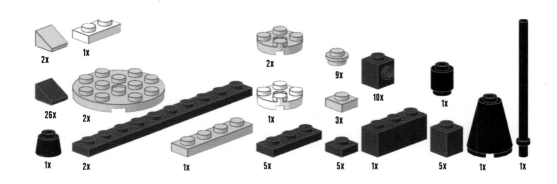

1

2

3

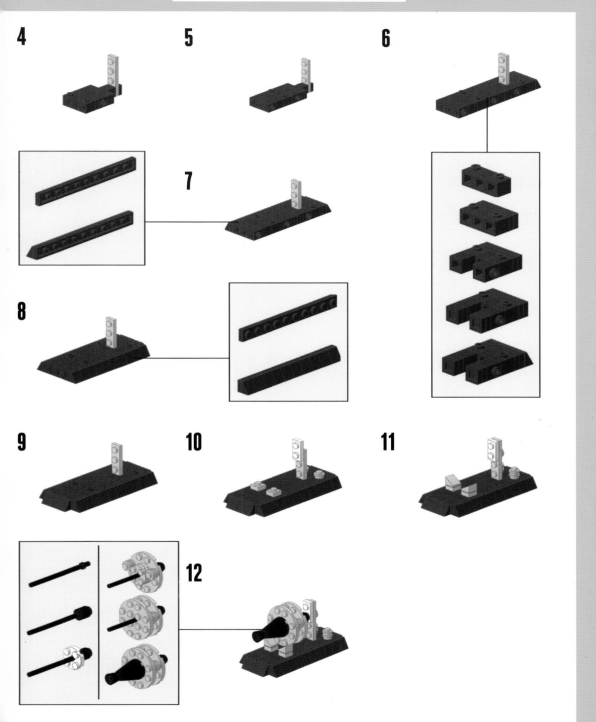

4

5

6

7

8

9

10

11

12

VICTORIAN ENGLAND, 1837-1901

Queen Victoria had one of the longest reigns in British history, and with it came a period of peace, stability and invention. The Victorian period was rich in culture, producing authors such as Arthur Conan Doyle, Charles Dickens and the Brontë sisters. Technology blossomed with the discovery of electricity, telegraphs and photography. The health of the nation improved with the introduction of anaesthetics and antiseptics, and for the first time ever children were required to go to school. It wasn't such a great time for some, however – Jack the Ripper was an infamous figure in Victorian London. He allegedly murdered 11 women and was never caught, though theories abound as to his true identity.

20th Century and Beyond

Invention of Radio, 1895

Guglielmo Marconi was an Italian inventor who pioneered long-distance radio. Although he didn't discover radio waves, he did bring them to the masses. In December 1902, he became the first person to send a radio signal more than 3,220km (2,000 miles) across the Atlantic – going from North America to Europe! Marconi's radios were rapidly installed on ships travelling the Atlantic Ocean because – for the first time – it gave them the ability to communicate with land. The Marconi Company provided all of the operators and equipment, such as this wireless Morse code set, to many ships, including the ill-fated *Titanic*. In fact, were it not for a Marconi radio summoning help, all of the *Titanic*'s passengers and crew would have likely died at sea.

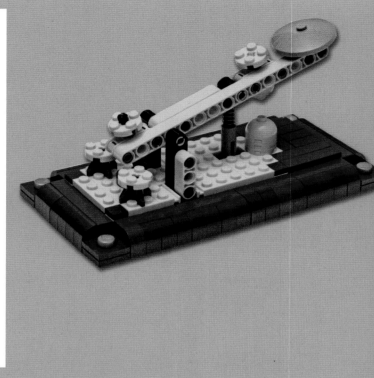

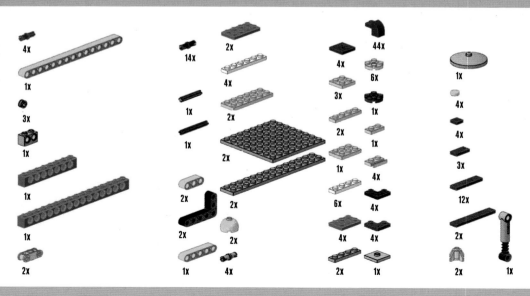

4x

14x

2x

44x

4x

1x

6x

1x

3x

4x

1x

4x

1x

1x

3x

4x

1x

2x

2x

1x

1x

1x

4x

2x

2x

6x

4x

12x

1x

2x

2x

4x

4x

2x

1x

2x

1x

2x

1x

1

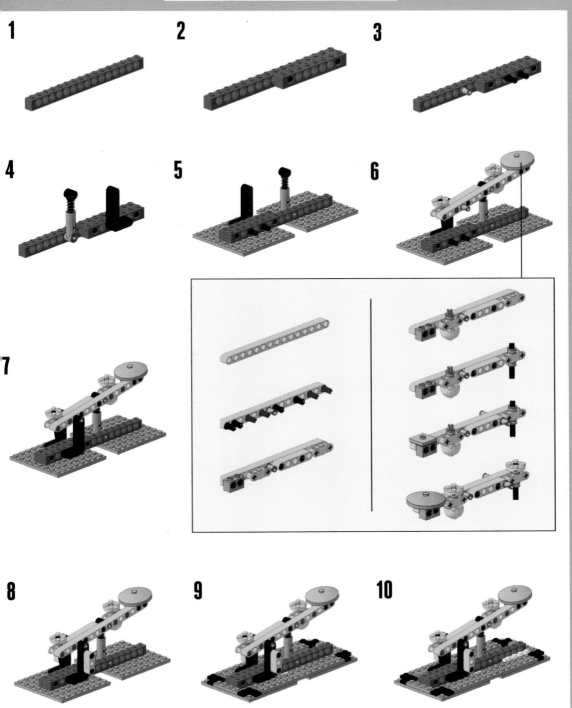

2

3

4

5

6

7

8

9

10

11

12

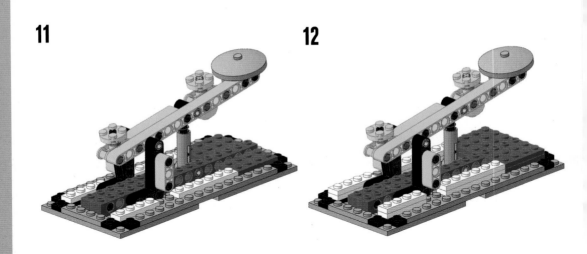

13

14

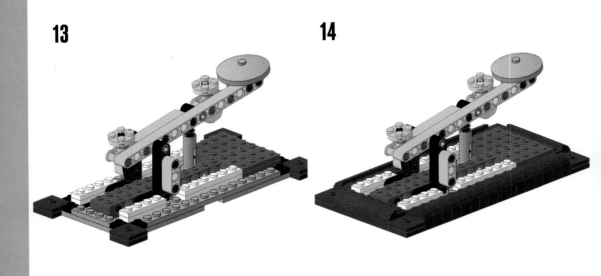

15

16

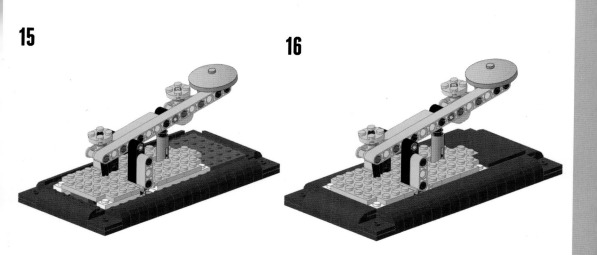

17

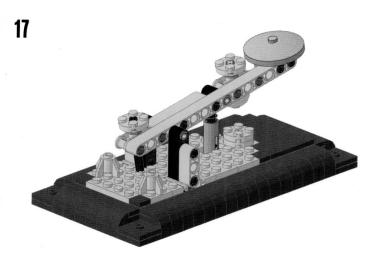

WRIGHT BROTHERS' FIRST FLIGHT, 1903

In 1903, Walter and Wilbur Wright flew this machine 36.5m (120ft). That's less than the wingspan of a modern jumbo jet, but it was still very important. This was the first time that an aeroplane that is heavier than air flew in a controlled flight – the Wright brothers had begun the age of aviation. More than just being the inventors of flight, these men also perfected the controls necessary to steer an aircraft and control its roll. The combination of these developments, as well as efficient engines and propellers, led the twentieth century into its obsession with flight, which continues today!

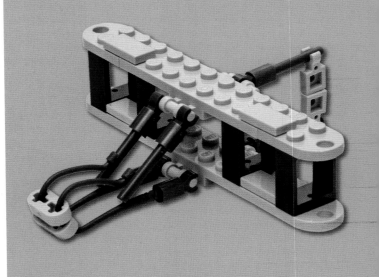

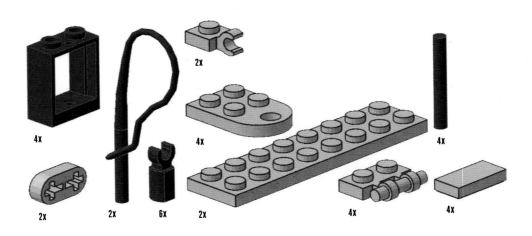

4x   2x   4x   4x

2x   2x   6x   2x   4x   4x

1

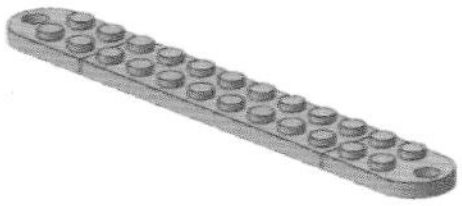

2

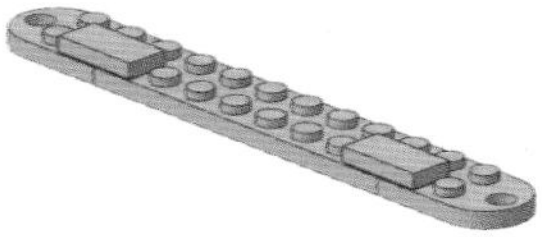

3

4

5

6

7

8

9

10

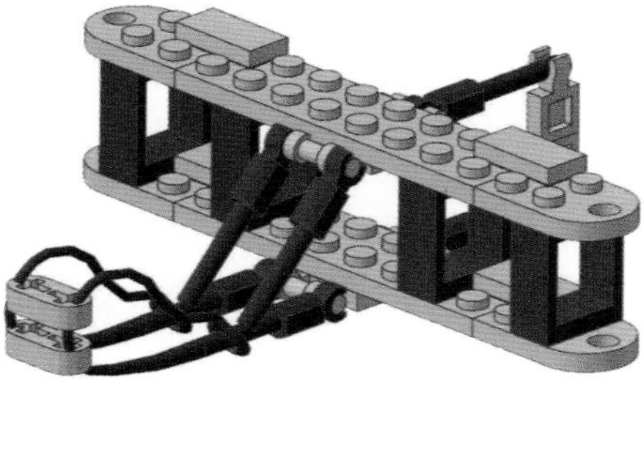

ALBERT EINSTEIN'S THEORY OF RELATIVITY, 1905

Einstein's theory of relativity is considered to be one of the most important theories in modern physics. It's actually two theories – those of general and special relativity. Special relativity is a theory that space and time are connected and can in many circumstances be treated as parts of the same thing. General relativity is a theory of gravity. Whereas we might not all understand the theories themselves, we have almost certainly used them. GPS navigation works because of the theory of relativity, so without Einstein's theories, we'd still be using maps and our smartphones would have no idea where the nearest shops are!

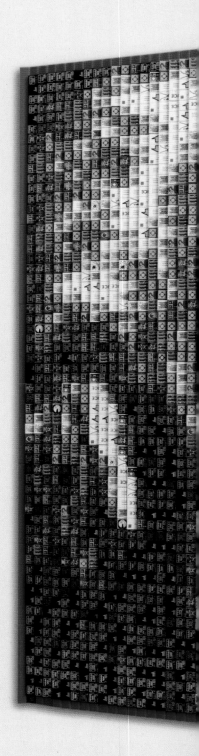

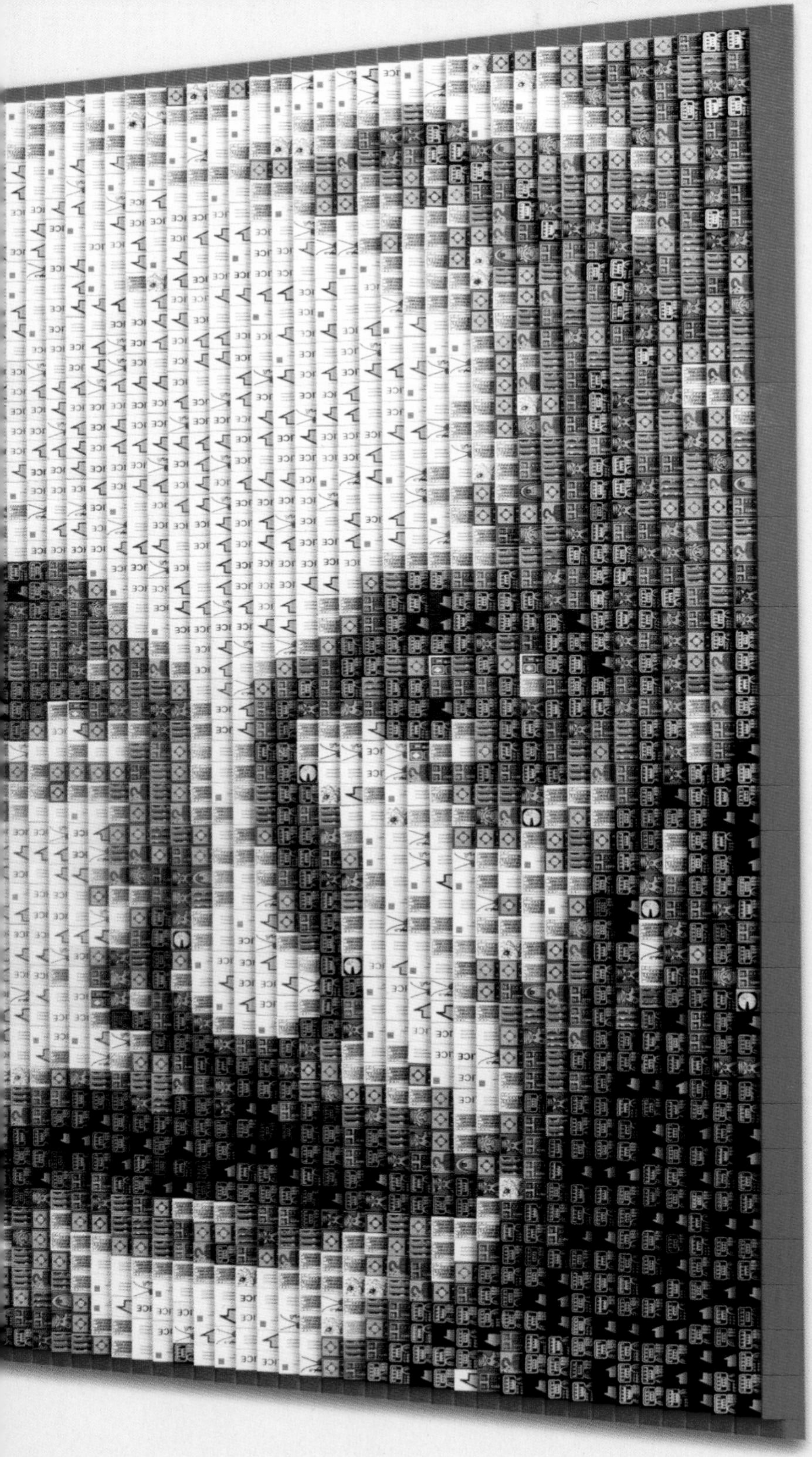

RMS Titanic Sinks, 1912

When she was launched, the *Titanic* was considered 'unsinkable'. Sadly, today her name is synonymous with disaster. In 1912, *Titanic* left Southampton, UK, on her first-ever voyage. She was meant to arrive in New York, but just four days later, her voyage was cut short. Late at night, the lookout suddenly saw an approaching iceberg. It was too late to avoid hitting it, and the collision tore a hole in the ship underneath the waterline. At the time, there was no requirement to carry enough lifeboats for all the passengers, and more than 1,500 passengers and crew would drown before they could be saved. The world's fascination with this incredible ship increased enormously following the release of the 1997 box office hit *Titanic*, starring Leonardo DiCaprio and Kate Winslet.

RMS TITANIC

Following the ship's collision with the iceberg, five of the ship's watertight compartments were breached, and this meant only one possible outcome – the ship would sink. After the sinking of the *Titanic* a number of important safety measures were put in place to help ensure such disasters never happened again. These included simple things we now take for granted, such as making sure that there are enough lifeboats for all the passengers. This model is too small to hold any lifeboats, so check no one's aboard before sailing it!

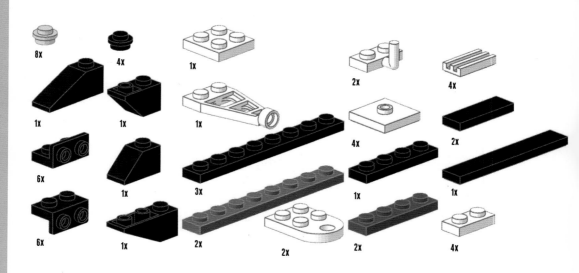

8x

4x

1x

2x

4x

1x

1x

1x

4x

2x

6x

1x

3x

1x

1x

6x

1x

2x

2x

2x

4x

1

2

3

4

5

6

7

8

9

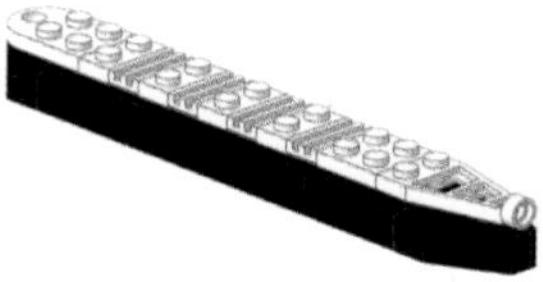

10

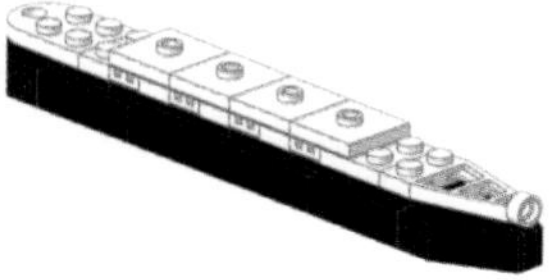

11

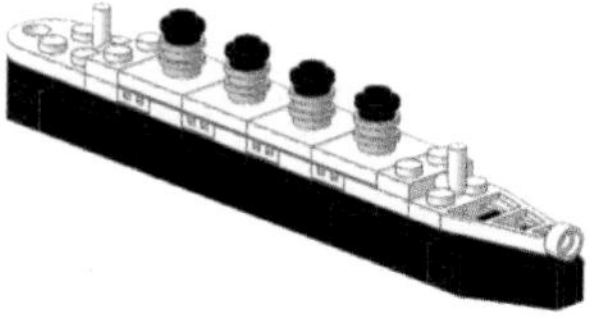

WOMEN'S SUFFRAGE MOVEMENT, C.1900

Although democracy has been in existence for a very long time, throughout much of history voting has been restricted to a small number of people, largely men. In the early 1900s, the suffrage movement in England was frustrated that women were not allowed to vote. Suffragettes there campaigned for equality by both protesting and carrying out militant actions to highlight their cause. They eventually won, and in 1928 women finally received the exact same rights as men. In the United States the same legislation was passed earlier, in 1920, following decades of nationwide campaigning.

CONSTRUCTION OF THE PANAMA CANAL, 1903-1914

Constructing the Panama Canal was in itself a marvel of engineering. To cut such a long and deep passage, more than 150 million cubic metres (5 billion cubic feet) of rock, soil and mud had to be extracted. By the time it was completed in 1914, it had cost the United States the equivalent of $8.6 billion to build. The United States wasn't the first to try to build such a monumental structure though – it took over an earlier failed French attempt, and records show that the idea for a shipping canal dates as far back as 1534. It wouldn't be until modern heavy machinery and proper healthcare measures for those who worked on its construction became available that the canal would be completed. Today, it is often referred to as one of the Wonders of the Modern World.

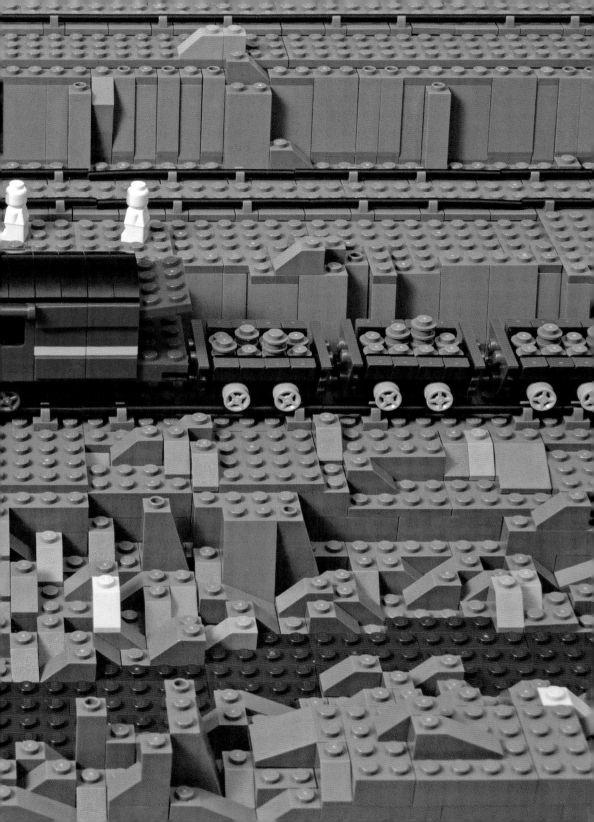

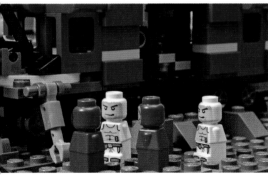

PANAMA CANAL STEAM SHOVEL, C.1910

Not only one of the Modern Wonders of the World, the Panama Canal changed transport history forever. By driving a canal from the Atlantic to the Pacific Ocean, the journey times for ships were slashed from long, dangerous months to just two weeks. Cutting journey times meant that all of a sudden new shipping routes were possible. Europe and the eastern coast of the United States could buy goods from Japan and China, while oil could be drilled in California and sold to the East. Even 100 years on, 5 percent of the world's ocean traffic still goes through the Panama Canal. This American steam shovel would have been used to excavate the area through which the canal was to be built.

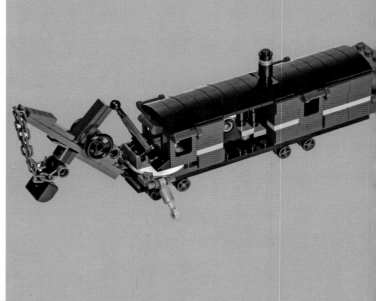

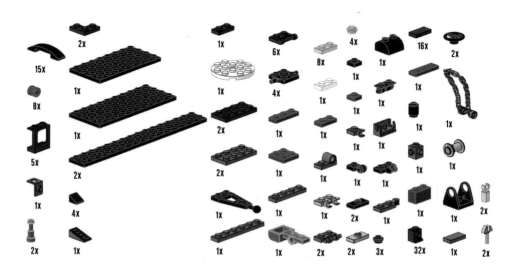

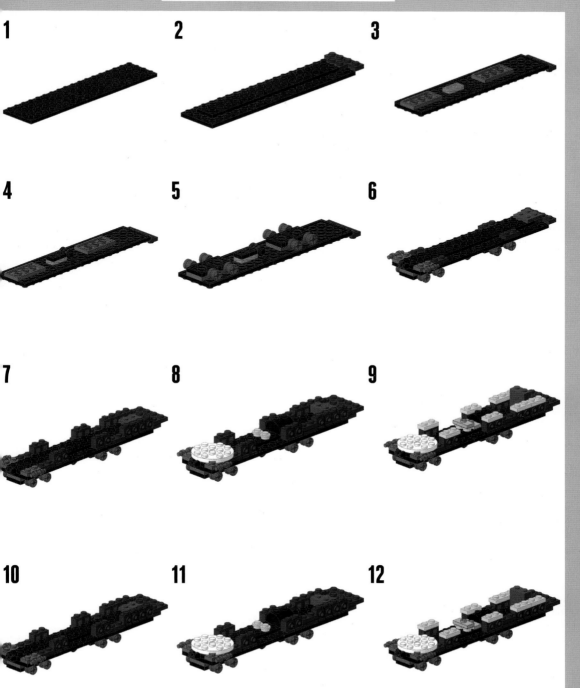

13

14

15

16

17

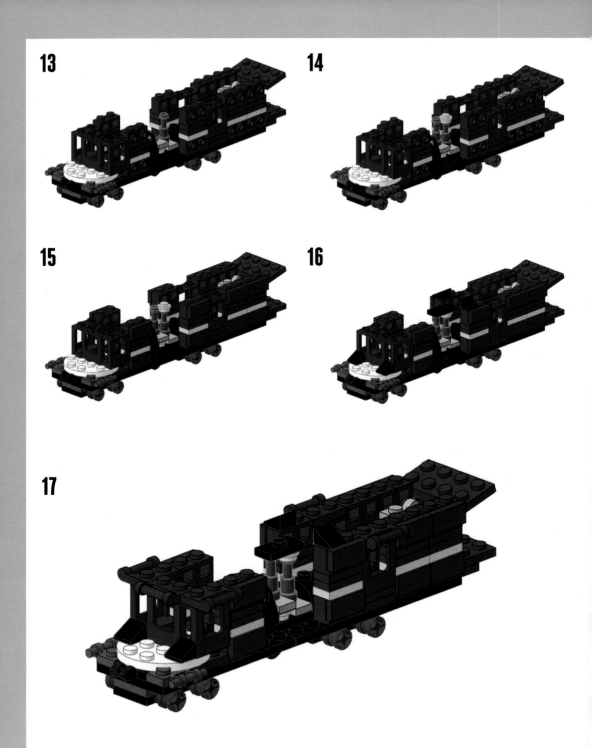

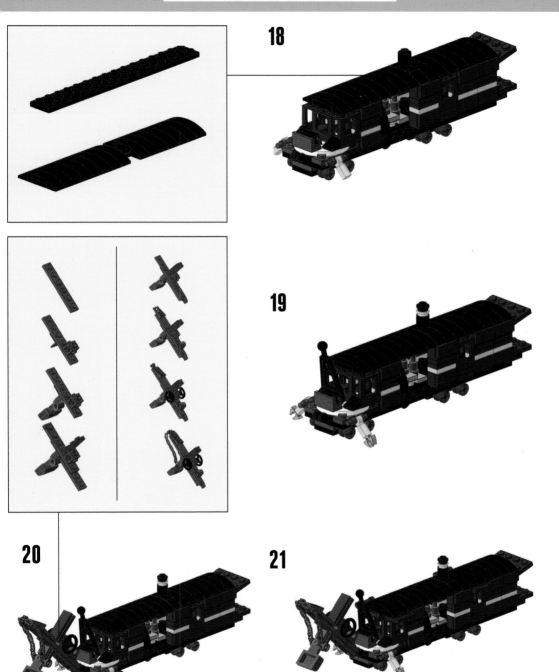

18

19

20

21

BOLSHEVIK REVOLUTION, 1917

The Bolshevik Revolution – symbolised by this hammer and sickle – sparked the beginning of communist leadership in the Union of Soviet Socialist Republics (U.S.S.R.). After defeat in World War I, Russia was ready for a change, and the people rallied around Lenin, the leader of the Bolshevik party. The creation of the U.S.S.R. would change the world forever. After World War II, the standoff between the United States and the U.S.S.R., known as the 'Cold War', also led to rapid technological developments on both sides, which has given us everything from computers to GPS navigation.

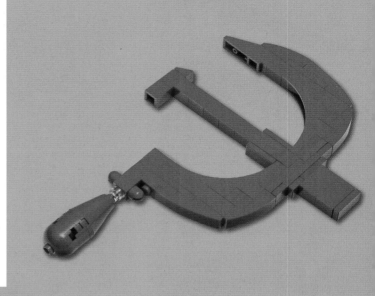

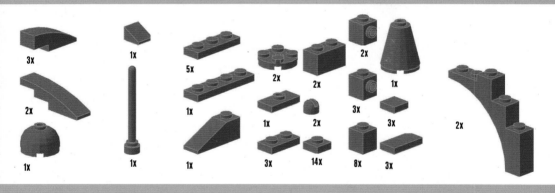

3x   1x   5x   2x   2x   2x

2x   1x   1x   3x   1x   3x   2x

1x   1x   1x   3x   14x   8x   3x

1   **2**   **3**

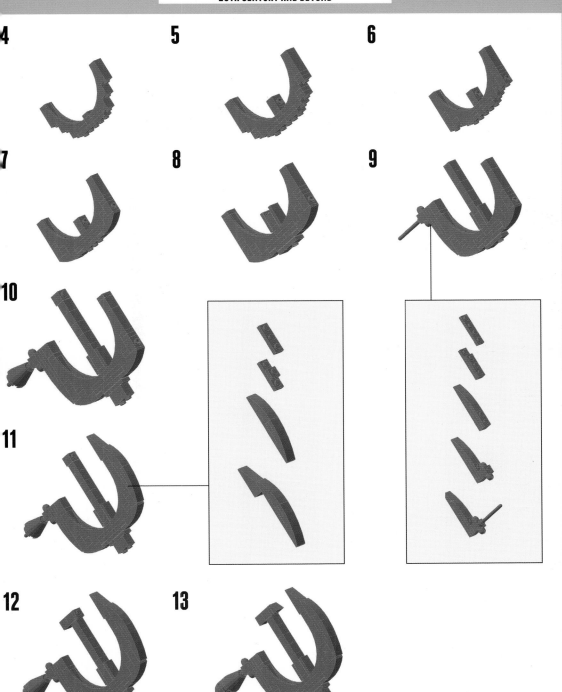

Peace Treaty of Versailles, 1919

The Treaty of Versailles marked the end of one of the deadliest wars in history, World War I. Known at the time as the Great War, it drew in all of the world's powerful nations in a way no other conflict had ever done before. Exactly five years after the assassination of Archduke Franz Ferdinand of Austria which sparked the fighting, the German government agreed to sign a peace treaty to officially end the war. Agreeing on such a complex document was no easy task, though — it took more than six months to finalise the treaty.

FIRST 'TALKIE' FILM RELEASED, 1927

Can you imagine going to watch a movie, but not being able to hear anyone talk? Until 1927, every film was like that. *The Jazz Singer* was the first-ever full-length film to have synchronised dialogue, though it only amounted to two minutes in total, plus six songs. It told the story of a Jewish boy who wanted to follow his dreams of becoming a jazz singer. The film was one of the most expensive made at the time, but the gamble worked. Back then, people thought that talkies would never take over completely. How wrong they were!

DISCOVERY OF PENICILLIN, 1928

Alexander Fleming discovered penicillin by accident, but its impact on the world has been massive. Before its introduction, you could die from a simple infection or even just a small wound. Penicillin was the first drug to be mass-produced to battle bacterial diseases and infections. All of a sudden, instead of the possibility of an amputation, your infection could be treated quickly and easily with a small injection. It's impossible to estimate its true impact, but it's likely that Fleming's discovery has saved more than 200 million lives in the last 90-odd years.

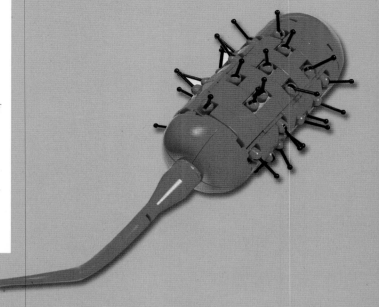

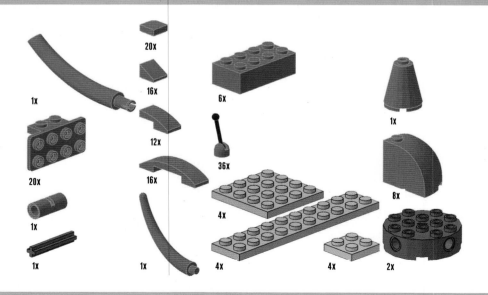

1

2

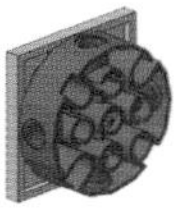

3

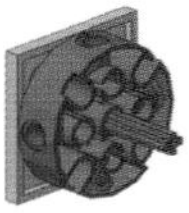

4

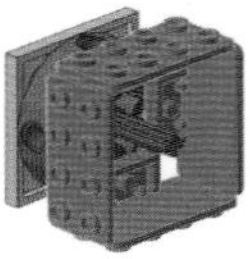

5

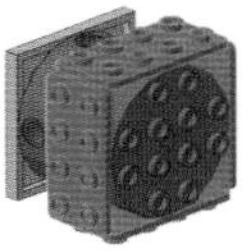

6

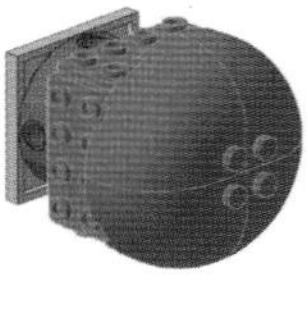

7

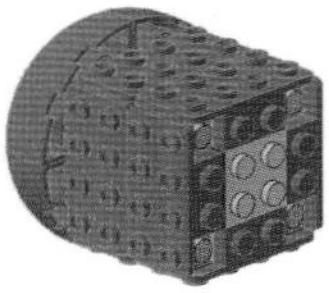

8

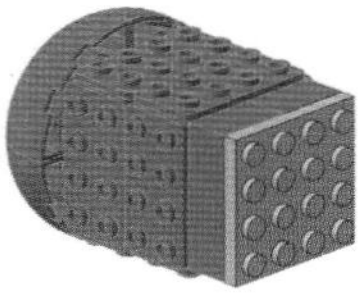

9

10

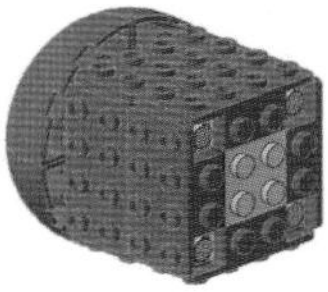

11

12

13

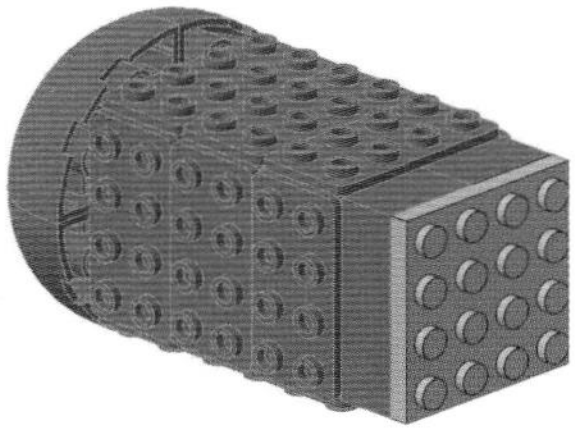

14

15

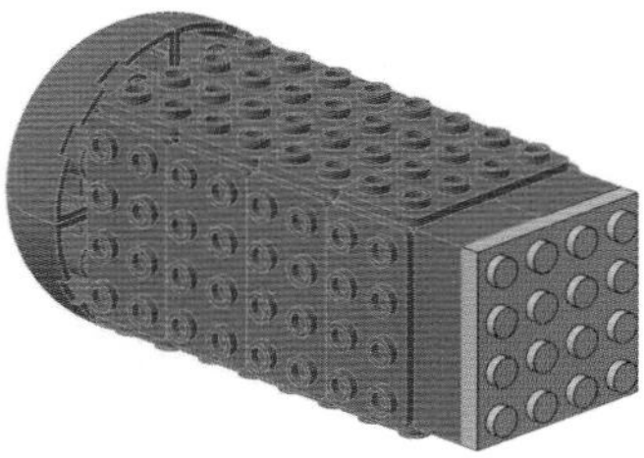

16

17

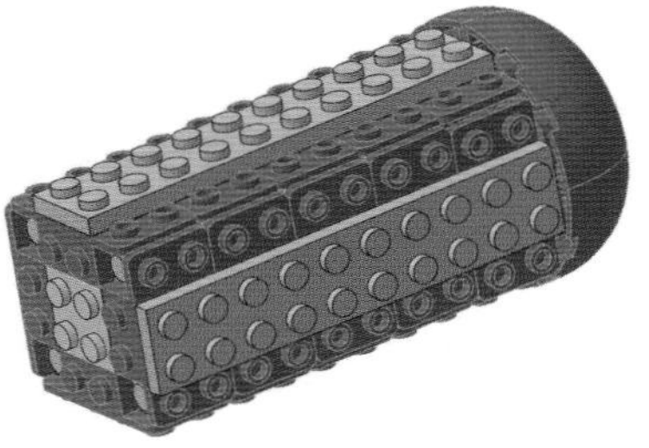

18

19

20

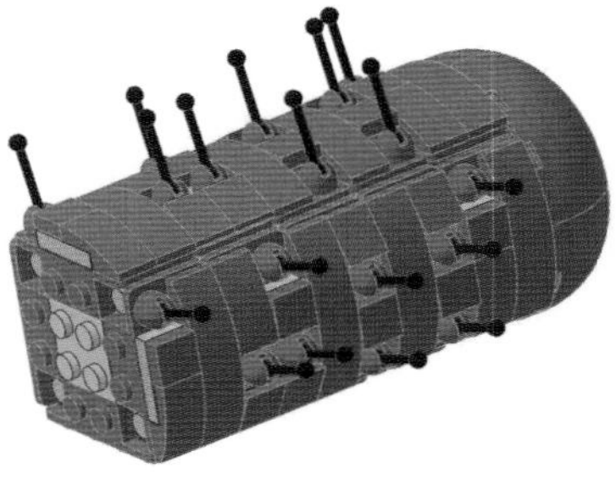

21

22

23

24

25

26

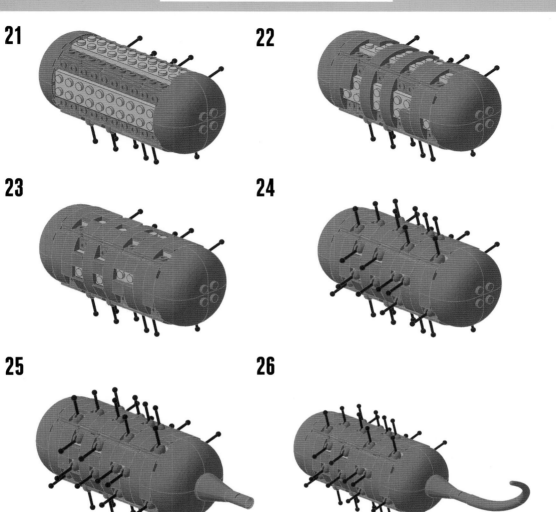

GANDHI'S HUNGER STRIKE AND INDEPENDENCE OF INDIA, 1932

Mahatma Gandhi is regarded as the father of modern India and a leading figure in the fight for political change. Born in British-ruled India, he led the country to its independence in 1947. Less well known was his fight for women's rights in India and his early activism in South Africa, where there are statues in his honour today. His use of non-violent tactics confused his critics at the time, but he has been seen as a role model ever since.

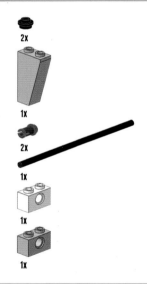

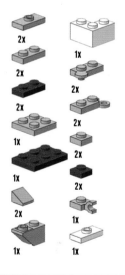

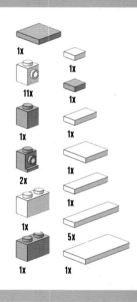

1

2

3

4

5

6

7

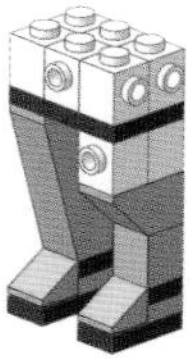

8

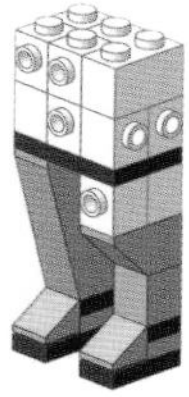

9

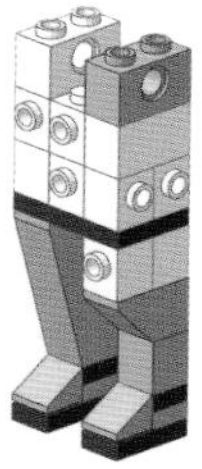

10

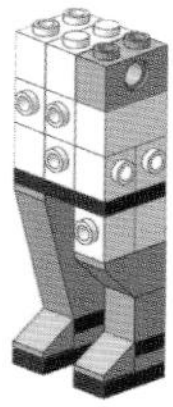

11

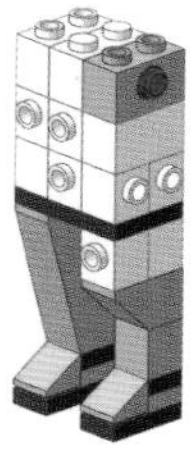

12

13

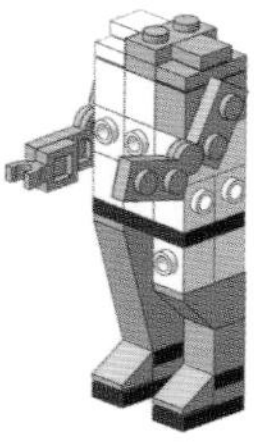

14

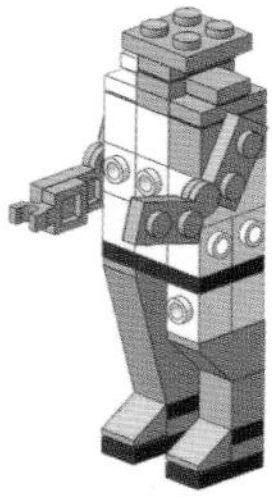

15

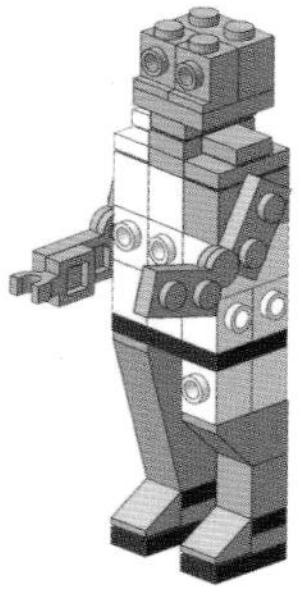

16

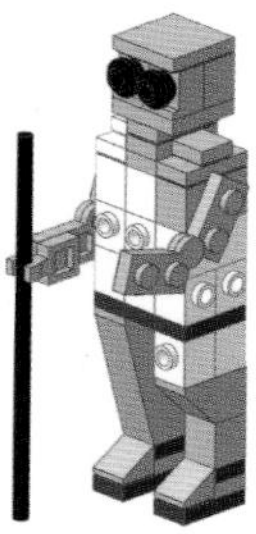

17

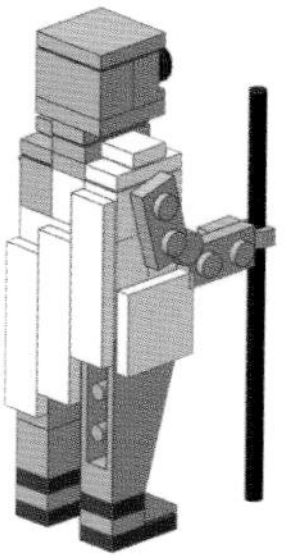

18

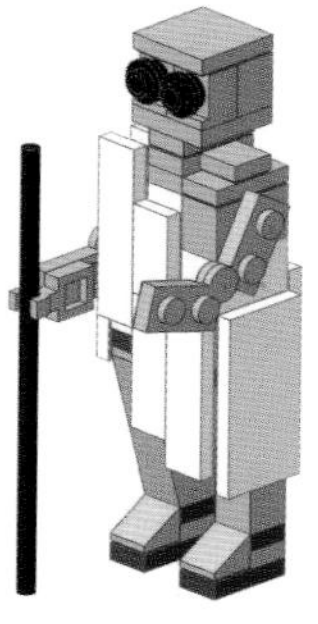

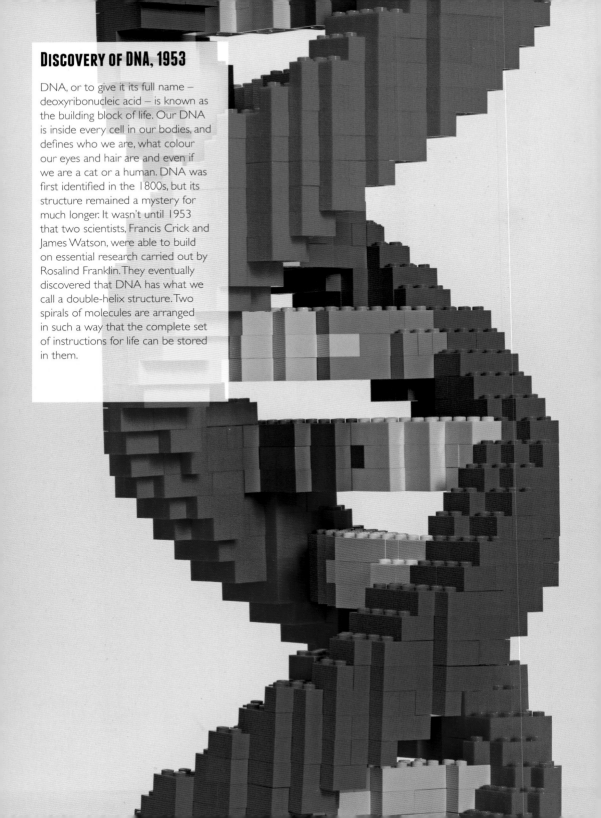

DISCOVERY OF DNA, 1953

DNA, or to give it its full name —
deoxyribonucleic acid — is known as
the building block of life. Our DNA
is inside every cell in our bodies, and
defines who we are, what colour
our eyes and hair are and even if
we are a cat or a human. DNA was
first identified in the 1800s, but its
structure remained a mystery for
much longer. It wasn't until 1953
that two scientists, Francis Crick and
James Watson, were able to build
on essential research carried out by
Rosalind Franklin. They eventually
discovered that DNA has what we
call a double-helix structure. Two
spirals of molecules are arranged
in such a way that the complete set
of instructions for life can be stored
in them.

MARTIN LUTHER KING'S 'I HAVE A DREAM' SPEECH, 1963

Although the United States banned slavery in 1865, racism continued. Black Americans were still subject to different rules and restrictions than their white neighbours, and were still treated as an underclass. Almost 100 years later, in 1963, civil rights activist Martin Luther King, Jr. took to the podium at the Lincoln Memorial in Washington, D.C. He spoke to more than 250,000 supporters who had joined him in a march calling for civil and economic equality in the United States. His speech is widely considered to be one of the most important in American history, and the opening words are known to everyone: 'I have a dream...'

Apollo 11 Moon Landing, 1969

On July 20, 1969, humans did
something they had never done
before. For the first time ever, a
person set foot on something other
than Earth. Astronauts Neil Armstrong
and Buzz Aldrin landed on the moon.
It was just eight short years after the
then-president of the United States,
John F. Kennedy, had set the challenge.
Landing people on the moon changed
our view of the Earth forever. For the
first time, we could look back towards
our planet and see it hanging in space.
One of the most famous photographs
of all time, 'The Blue Marble', was
taken by one of the lunar missions
that followed – and showed just how
fragile our planet is.

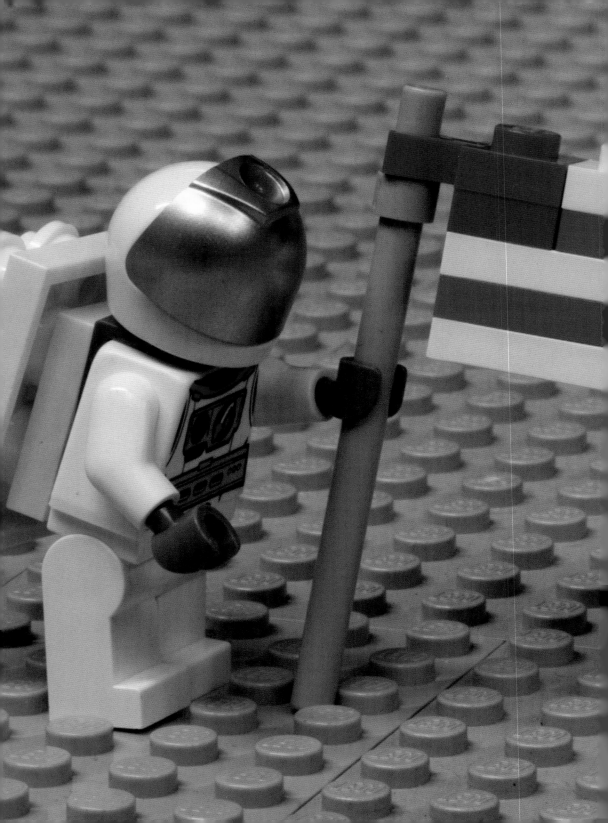

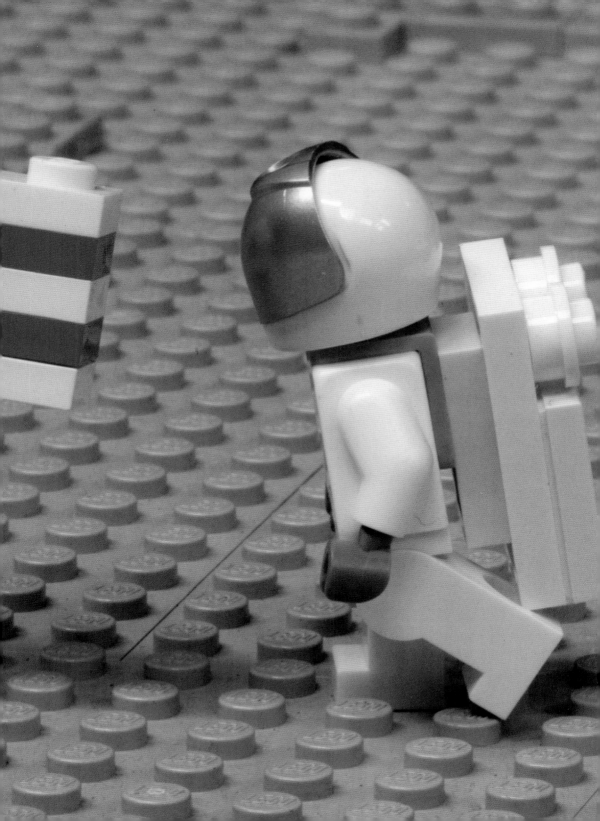

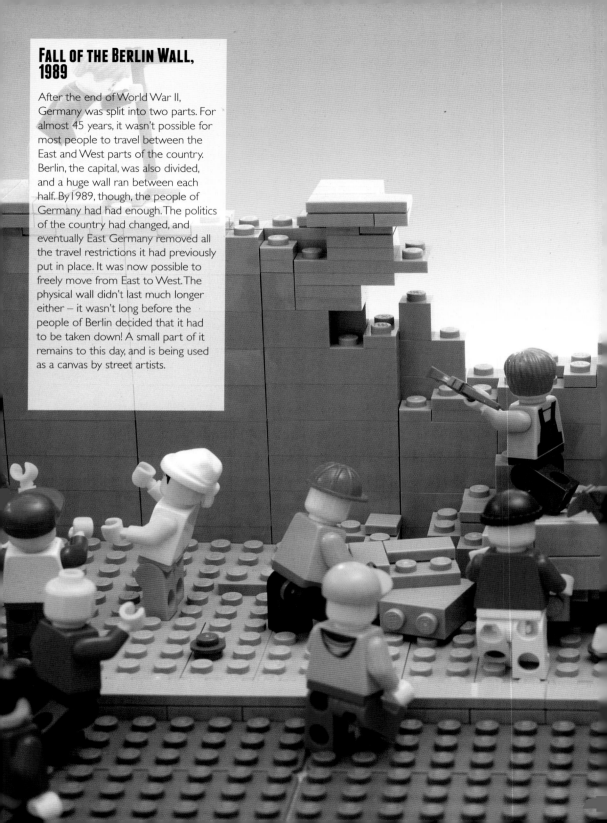

FALL OF THE BERLIN WALL, 1989

After the end of World War II, Germany was split into two parts. For almost 45 years, it wasn't possible for most people to travel between the East and West parts of the country. Berlin, the capital, was also divided, and a huge wall ran between each half. By 1989, though, the people of Germany had had enough. The politics of the country had changed, and eventually East Germany removed all the travel restrictions it had previously put in place. It was now possible to freely move from East to West. The physical wall didn't last much longer either — it wasn't long before the people of Berlin decided that it had to be taken down! A small part of it remains to this day, and is being used as a canvas by street artists.

NELSON MANDELA BECOMES PRESIDENT OF SOUTH AFRICA, 1994

In 1994, something amazing happened. Nelson Mandela became the president of South Africa. That doesn't sound amazing, except that he was the first black South African president elected by people of any skin colour. Before this, South Africa operated a system called 'apartheid', where anyone who wasn't white couldn't vote in an election. Nelson Mandela fought against this all his life and was imprisoned for 27 years because of his campaigning. He won his long fight in the end. Less than five years after being released from prison, the people of South Africa used democratic ballot boxes like this one to vote for change, and made him president.

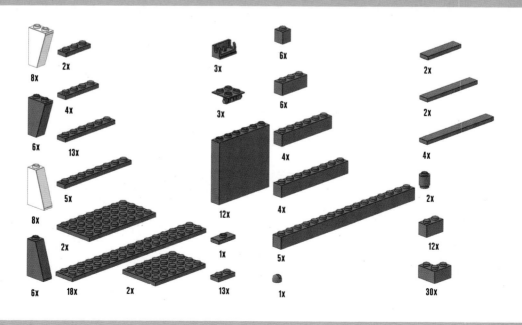

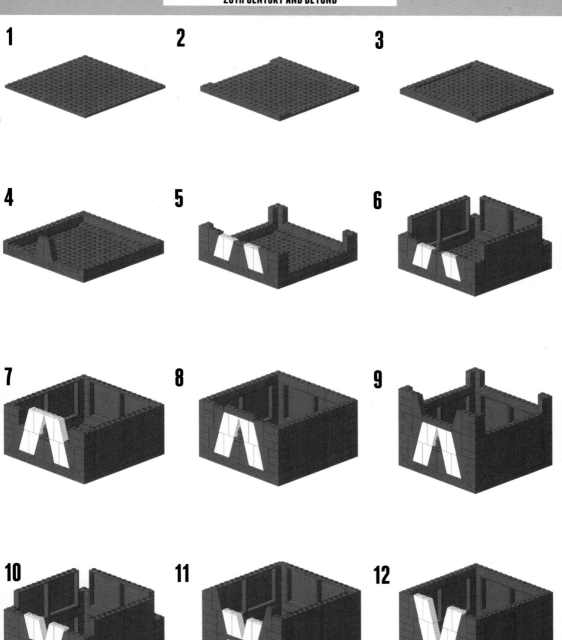

13

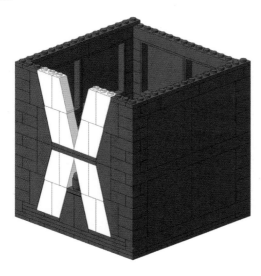

14

15

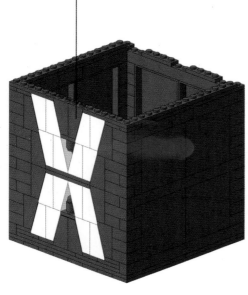

16

17

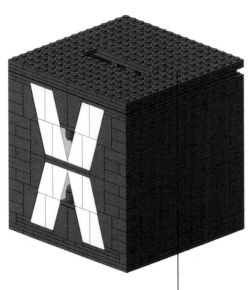

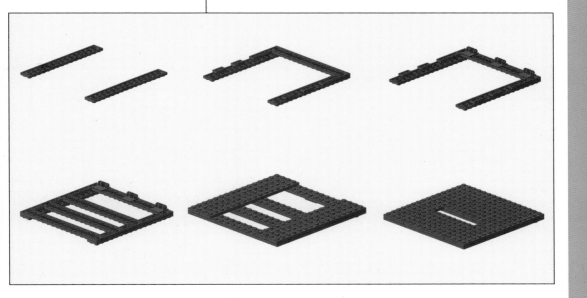

Hong Kong Handover, 1997

In the eighteenth and nineteenth centuries, it was common for European nations to have colonies. Explorers from Spain, The Netherlands, Great Britain and other countries would travel to the other side of the world and claim land for their country. Although some countries still have colonies, most have long since returned these lands. One of the last colonies to be returned by the British was Hong Kong. A large part of what is today known as Hong Kong was given to Britain on a 99-year lease, which ran out in 1997. After a period of negotiation, the territories were handed back to China in a ceremony that was broadcast worldwide and is widely regarded as marking the end of the British Empire.

INAUGURATION OF PRESIDENT BARACK OBAMA, 2009

The American Civil War was fought over the rights of black Americans. One hundred years later, Martin Luther King addressed a rally to continue the fight for equality. In 2009, another momentous thing happened – the United States swore into office its first-ever black president. Almost 38 million people across the country watched his inauguration, which was also widely seen throughout the world. Barack Obama was sworn in before the largest-ever audience – an estimated 1.8 million people.

ROYAL WEDDING OF PRINCE WILLIAM AND CATHERINE MIDDLETON, 2011

Throughout history, countries have come together or been thrown apart by kings and queens. It sometimes seems like this is all ancient history, but many countries around the world still retain their royal families as heads of state. So, when a royal prince decides to marry, it's still a huge occasion! One such occasion was the wedding of Prince William, Duke of Cambridge and the grandson of the Queen of England, to Catherine Middleton. The 2011 event took the whole world by storm. The first British royal wedding to occur in the Internet age meant that an estimated 72 million people watched live on YouTube as the couple wed.

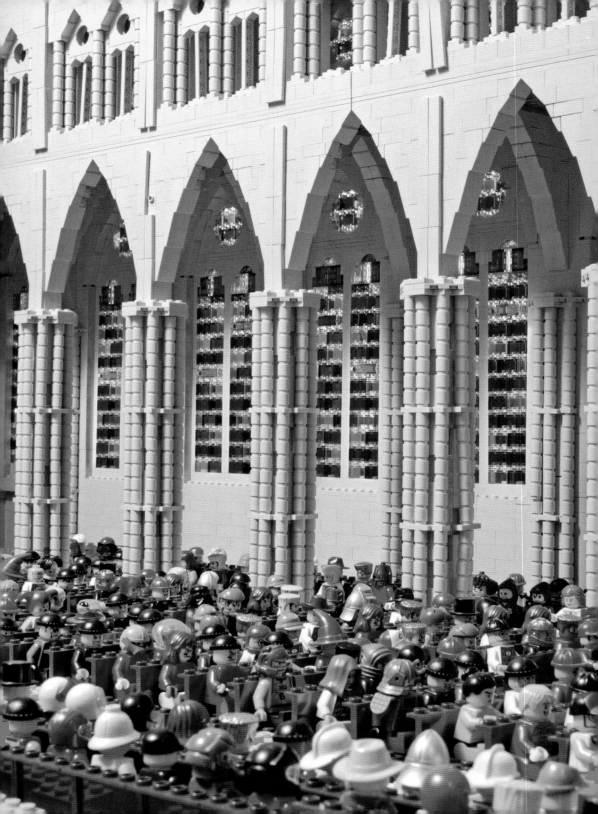

INDEX

CREDITS

Fraser Dallachy is a researcher in historical linguistics at the University of Glasgow. As an Adult Fan of LEGO® (AFOL), he enjoys building models relating to exploration and adventure.

Andrew Danieli has been building as an AFOL since 2007. He's always been interested in maritime history, and the *Mayflower* was an excuse to try his hand at a more realistic hull design. Andrew works as a software engineer for a global IT company, and has a degree in computer systems engineering.

Alastair Disley is a professional LEGO builder, architectural historian and musician. Previously a university lecturer, he lives in the Scottish Borders, UK, with his young family.

Teresa 'Kitty' Elsmore was a LEGO fan as a child and continues to enjoy creating models with LEGO bricks today. Her passion is for organising natural forms and all the little details that bring a scene to life. Since their marriage in 2005, Teresa and Warren Elsmore have collaborated on a number of projects, and she is responsible for many of the intricate details in the minifig scenes.

Warren Elsmore is an artist in LEGO bricks based in Edinburgh, UK. He has been in love with the little plastic bricks since the age of four and now spends his days creating amazing LEGO models. After 15 years in a successful IT career, in 2012 Warren moved to working full time with LEGO bricks, helping companies realise their dreams in plastic. Warren's bestselling first book (*Brick City*) was released in 21 languages to critical acclaim and has been followed by a range of books, each recreating parts of the world we inhabit in plastic bricks.

Exhibitions of Warren's first two books (*Brick City* and *Brick Wonders*) have toured the UK, entertaining hundreds of thousands of children of all ages. In 2015, Warren co-launched 'BRICK' – the largest LEGO fan event in the UK and one of the largest in the world. For more information, please visit *warrenelsmore.com*.

Alex Eylar is a writer from Oakland, California, and has been building with LEGO since his childhood. Since moving to Los Angeles, Alex spends his days in one of two spots: hunched over the computer writing, or sitting before the LEGO table building.

Arthur Gugick, a high school maths teacher, has been playing with LEGO continuously since 1967! Arthur specialises in LEGO landmarks from around the world and his LEGO mosaics of famous paintings and people are always in great demand.

Andrew Harvey is an AFOL based in Derby, UK. He has been building LEGO train models from an early age, particularly focusing on steam locomotives, and now works as a mechanical engineer for an international rail consultancy.

Kevin Hall is a professional LEGO brick artist and has been a graphic designer in the creative industry for the past 25 years. Originally from Australia, he now lives in Berkshire in the UK, where he runs his own company producing LEGO models. Kevin has been heavily involved in the LEGO community for the past 15 years, helping to start one of the first user groups in Australia.

Mario Sánchez has a degree in mathematics from Universidad de Salamanca, Spain. Since becoming a member of the Spanish HispaLUG association, Mario has displayed at many events throughout the country. You can enjoy all his creations at *brickrunner.es*.

Simon Pickard is an AFOL, married with five sons. He lives in Somerset, UK, and works as a build specialist for *Blocks Magazine*.

Erik Platt is 16 years old and has been building with LEGO as long as he can remember. He specialises in building miniature-scale military models as well as scenes from the American Revolutionary War.

The author would also like to thank builders **Gary Brooks** and **Michael Evans**.